Village

Photography, choreography and writing inspired by village life

First published in 2024
by Buckinghamshire Culture

First Edition

ISBN 978-1-0369-0605-4

Design by Eliza Hart
at Office Of Craig

Printed in England

with contributions from

Theo Clinkard
Camilla Greenwell
Ruth Quayle
Will Burns
Claire Fuller
&
Comments from Local Participants

Foreword

by
Bill Morris,
Julius Weinberg,
Co-Chairs,
Bucks Culture

Artists observe, interpret and imagine how we live in unique ways that surprise, inform and move us. We are delighted to have been able to invite five artists from photography, choreography, literature and poetry to engage with local communities and locations to explore our villages. Often adjacent to large cities, modern village life is often overlooked.

Village captures some of the spirit of these places, with images and stories rich with human feelings from moments of isolation to shared collective joy.

Introduction

by

Eckhard Thiemann

Creative Associate,
Bucks Culture

Buckinghamshire is a county of villages. Renowned for their beauty, historic relevance and unique identities, they form much of the county's identity for residents, visitors and tourists. Many feature as locations in films, TV and picture books. Some of the quintessential English iconography is encapsulated in these places. But villages also experience a great deal of transformation. They witness growth through new developments and housing estates, gentrification and rising house prices, changes in demographics, lack of transport links, and challenges to local high street economies.

Village shines a light on modern village life through photography, movement and writing. Choreographer Theo Clinkard and photographer Camilla Greenwell take their inspiration from Pieter Bruegel's famous and action-filled paintings of 16th century Flemish village life with their elevated viewpoints and ask what collectivism and communal village life looks like today. Local residents in Fairford Leys, Brill and Burnham were invited to take part in creating panoramic portraits of their villages. Their choreographed stagings create playful images that are part fantasy, part realistic portrait. Shot through with humour and incidental detail, these images capture 21st century villagers in a creative and collective act to be, imagine and perform themselves.

The writers Claire Fuller, Will Burns and Ruth Quayle spent time in each village, observing and using the location as a springboard for new imaginations. Ruth Quayle proposes a wondrous creation myth of a hilltop village in her fantastical children's story. Claire Fuller explores loneliness and search for companionship in two flash-fiction vignettes, in which romantic desire and horror uncomfortably meet. Will Burns reveals the typology of modern village design in a caustic poem, casting his analytical eye on a location that feels so familiar, yet so strange. Quotes from local participants add further nuance to the complex nature of villages.

In addition to the material in this book, *Village* included workshops with local writers and schools, creating more texts and images available on the Bucks Culture website.

Choreography & Image

by
Theo Clinkard

The *Village* photography project began with an inspired conversation with my creative producer, Rosalind Conlon and forms one part of a larger ongoing project that draws upon my love of the 16th century Flemish artist, Pieter Bruegel the Elder.

As a boy, Bruegel was introduced to me by my dad, Julian, who had a wonderful way of making his paintings come to life by encouraging me to feel my way around a scene, painting the wider context for me or simply drawing my eye to the evocative use of light.

As a choreographer, I find Bruegel's work to be deeply choreographic, the body is central in depicting emotion and experience while the chaos he captures is in fact beautifully composed and balanced. The core themes that underpin Bruegel's works, from the impact of the weather on our lives to the portrayal of community as a complex and diverse ecology, mean they still feel deeply relevant some 500 years later.

This project offered an exciting way to continue a collaborative relationship with photographer Camilla Greenwell. Together we sought to tell new stories with local folk by not just capturing each place and the people that live there, but the collective imagination of these communities.

In practice, it was a pure unexpected joy. It turned out that hundreds of adventurous people were up for the challenge of making a huge artwork with us. Dressed in something they would wear to work or for leisure activities, ready to suggest moves or scenes they could enact, they came together for a couple of hours to be creative with other people from their community. I am quite sure that these photos capture some of the most bizarre hours of all of our lives and I am so thankful for the enthusiasm each and every person brought to this adventure.

Bruegel's paintings offer us a portal-like window into the everyday lives of his local community and I hope that in years to come, the 10-day old baby that took part, can look back at these brilliant participants who recognised the power and joy of taking part in something collective and even find inspiration for their own creative future.

Photography

by
Camilla Greenwell

The

village

of

Brill

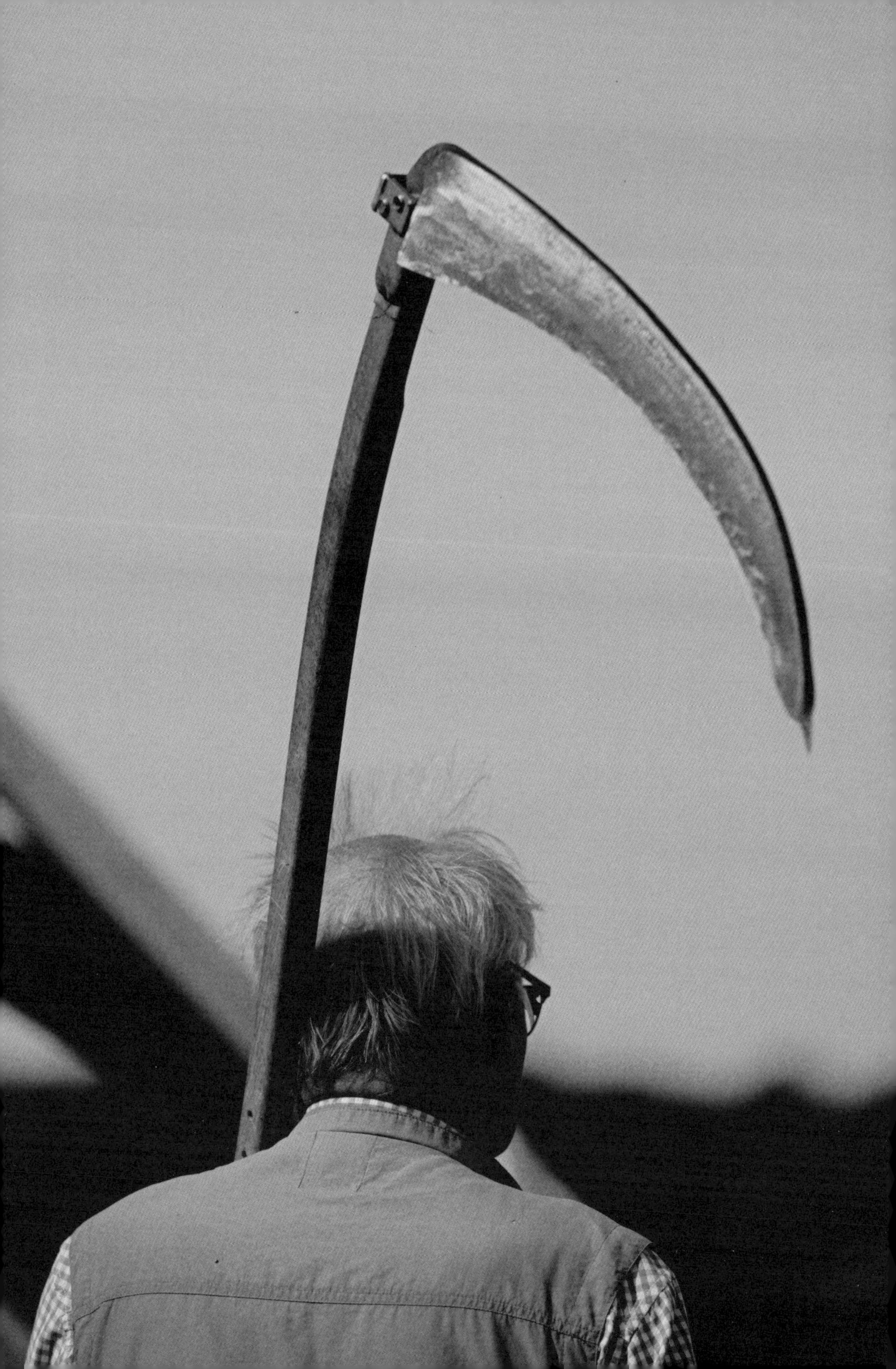

The Giant Who Picked Up A Village

by

Ruth Quayle

Once a long time ago in this small corner of the world lived a giant. This giant looked a bit like the trees and a lot like the grass and a teeny bit like the sky. She was very well camouflaged.

The people who lived in this small corner of the world had no idea the giant was there. This might not have mattered if she'd been a solitary sort of giant, but she wasn't. She wanted people to see her. She wanted to belong.

So, one day the giant climbed to the top of the nearest hill and gazed down at the land below. She saw grassy fields and dusty paths and streams that tinkled like glass. She saw a hunting forest that belonged to a king and a bottomless pool for catching ducks. She saw a windmill with sails that spun round and round like a party game. Then, at the edge of all this, she found what she was looking for. Houses. Animals. People.

A village.

The giant spent a long time looking at that village. She thought it was one of the loveliest things she'd ever seen. At first, she tried waving to the people below. But her waves sent clouds scudding across the sky like boats. A few people glanced up and frowned, but they did not notice the giant.

'Hello!' she shouted. 'I'm up here!'

Her deep voice blew apart the clouds, scattering them like dandelion clocks and sending snow to the village below. The snow magicked the village into a wonderland. Everybody was far too busy playing in it to notice the giant.

At this point she realised she was going to have to do more than wave and shout. She needed to put herself in the spotlight. Then they'd have to see her.

The giant stood on tippy toes and stretched her right arm all the way to the sun. She pulled it down so it shone directly on her.

But the sun melted the snow and made the villagers slow and sleepy. They put on wide-brimmed hats and lay under shady trees. When they looked up, they saw leaves and branches and acorns – but no giant.

The giant let go of the sun and sighed. I'll have to do something else to make them notice me, she thought.

She began to stomp her feet. Her stomps rumbled around the valley like thunder. Sheep scattered. Farmers shook their heads. Children ran indoors.

The giant sat down and put her head in her hands.

'Please look at me,' she said sadly. 'Just for once.'

A giant-sized tear appeared under her left eye. It ran down her cheek and landed with a splosh on the grass below. Another tear followed, and another, and soon a puddle of tears had pooled at the giant's feet.

For many days she sat and wept. The puddle at her feet became a pond and the pond began to trickle down the grassy slope. The trickle turned into a stream and the stream turned into a river. It flowed through the streets and snaked through the forest. Grassy fields were transformed into oceans.

Villagers looked anxiously out of their windows as the water rose above their doorsteps and lapped at their stairs. And then something truly awful started to happen. The buildings pulled and wrenched at their moorings. The village began to float away. People screamed.

Until this point the giant had been blinded by her own tears. She hadn't noticed the rising water. But when she heard the screaming, she looked down. And when she saw what was happening, she was horrified. She hadn't meant to cause a flood. She hadn't meant to frighten people.

She wiped away her tears. There was no time to waste.

Crouching on top of the hill she stretched down her hands. She picked up the houses and barns. She picked up the church and the school and the pubs. She picked up the windmill – taking extra care not to damage its sails. She gathered everything up in her generous arms and one by one she placed each of the buildings in safe, dry spots on top of the hill.

After this she lay down with her head on the windmill and fell into a lovely long sleep. When she woke up, the sky was full of stars. She wasn't sure if she'd been asleep for a few hours or a few years (giants are terrible timekeepers) but she couldn't help noticing that her knees and elbows had squished the ground whilst she slept, creating strange lumps and bumps.

Next to her feet, stretched higgledy-piggledy across the lumpy hillside, lay the village she had rescued. Smoke rose from chimneys, candles flickered in windows, and buildings snored in the moonlight. It was peaceful. It was safe.

The giant was pleased that the village was safe but sorry for all the trouble her tears had caused. She decided she couldn't stay in the place she had nearly destroyed. She decided to find somewhere new to live. But as she was walking away something made her shiver. It was a strange feeling; one she hadn't experienced before. She felt she was being watched.

At that moment she noticed the people. They were holding lanterns and parading around a huge bonfire. They were looking up. The giant wondered what they could be looking at. She leaned a little closer. And then she heard something.

'Thank you for saving our village! Thank you whoever you are!'

The giant rubbed her eyes. They couldn't be talking to her.

After all they couldn't see her.

Far below, the windmill creaked comfortingly and the bonfire crackled and the hillside echoed with the same wonderful words.

'Thank you!' sang the voices. 'THANK YOU!'

The giant's legs trembled. The people seemed to be talking to her. But how could she be sure? She thought for a long time and eventually she had an idea.

She cast her hands into the night sky and began to swirl them around as if she was conducting an enormous orchestra. She picked up the stars and sent them flying over the moon. She waved planets here, there and everywhere. She turned comets into glittering whirlpools. She made the sky twirl and spin and dance.

The people below applauded this magnificent display, and the giant swayed to the sound of their cheers. She looked across at the exploding sky and she looked down at the twinkling village, and she decided not to leave.

Instead, she promised to light up the skies next year and the year after that and every year since. And today, the villagers continue to thank the giant by lighting fires, carrying lanterns and looking up.

Because even though they can't see her, they know she is there, and this is where she belongs.

The End

"It's a great place to live,
with beautiful scenery and
a warm community."

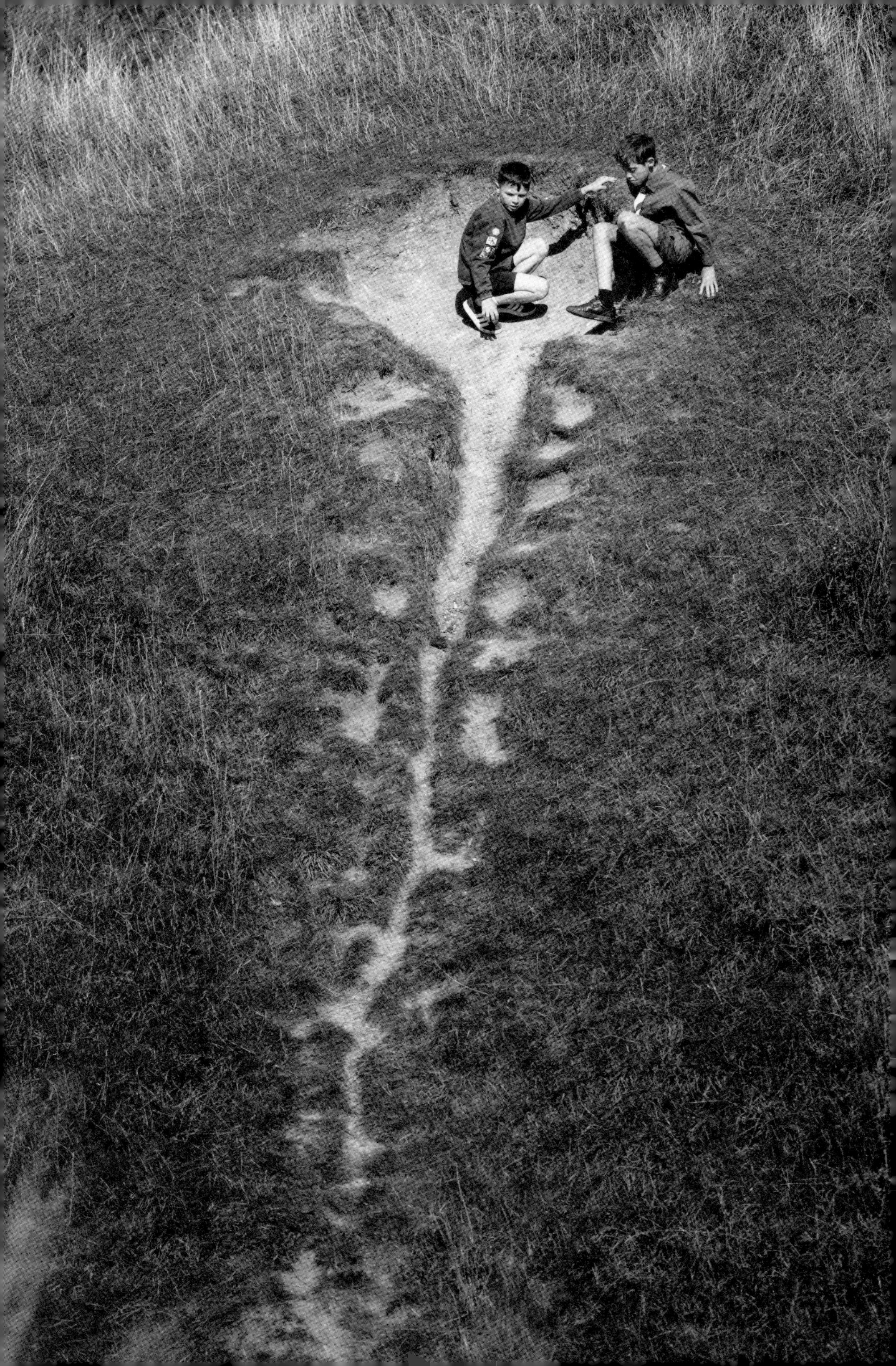

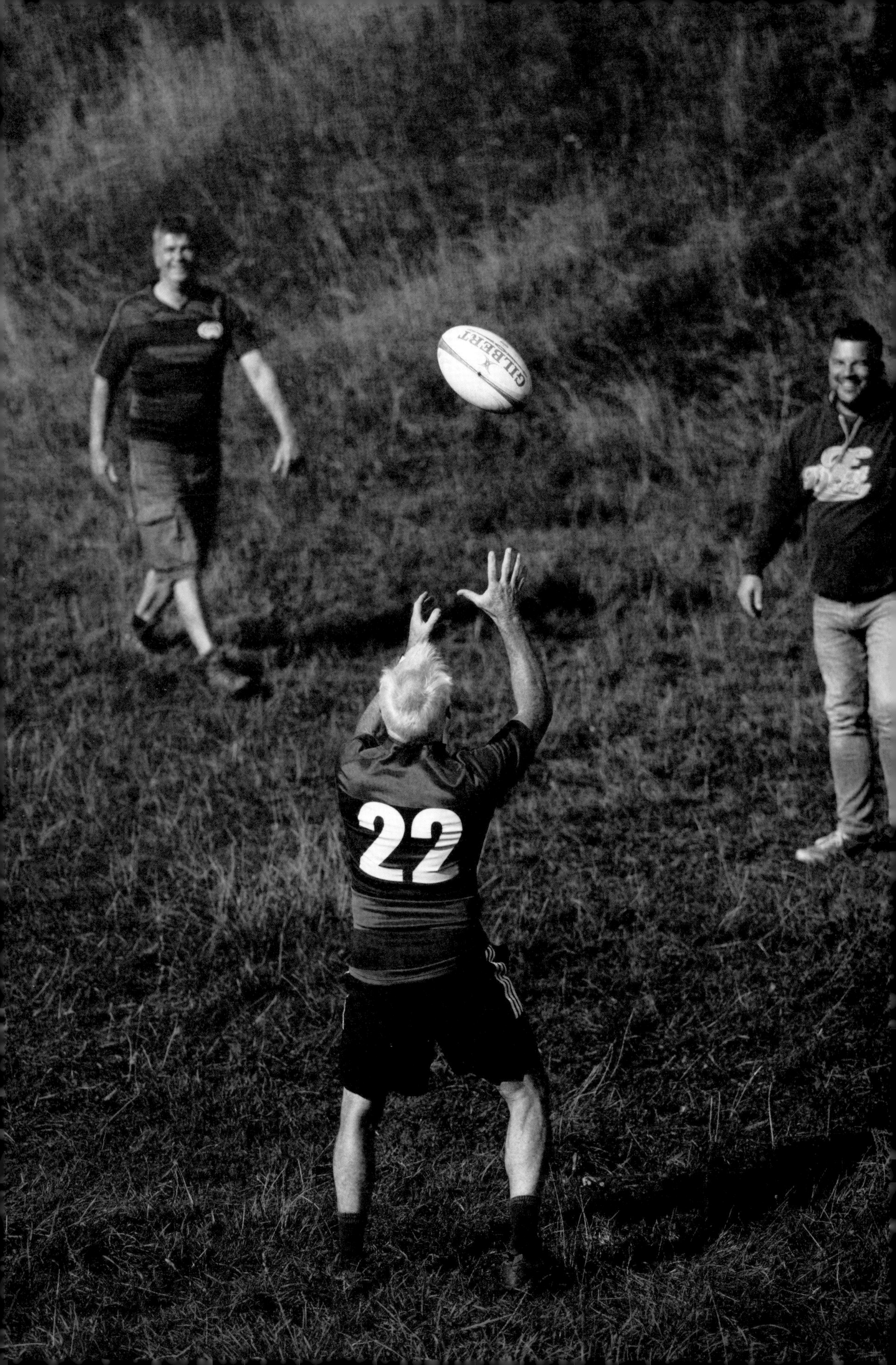
GILBERT
22

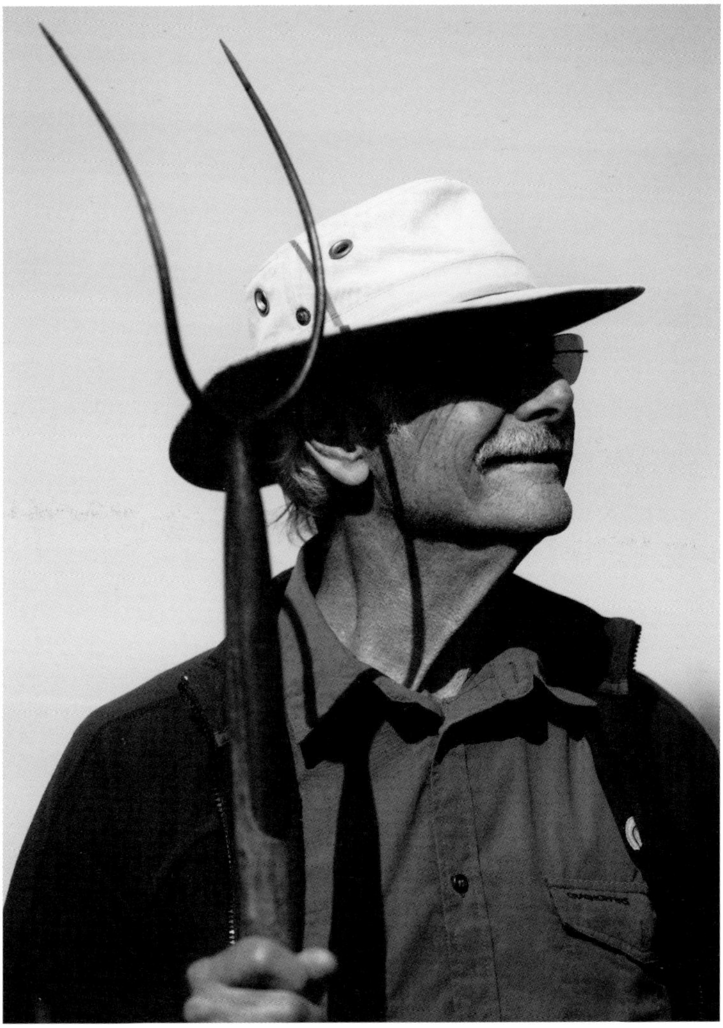

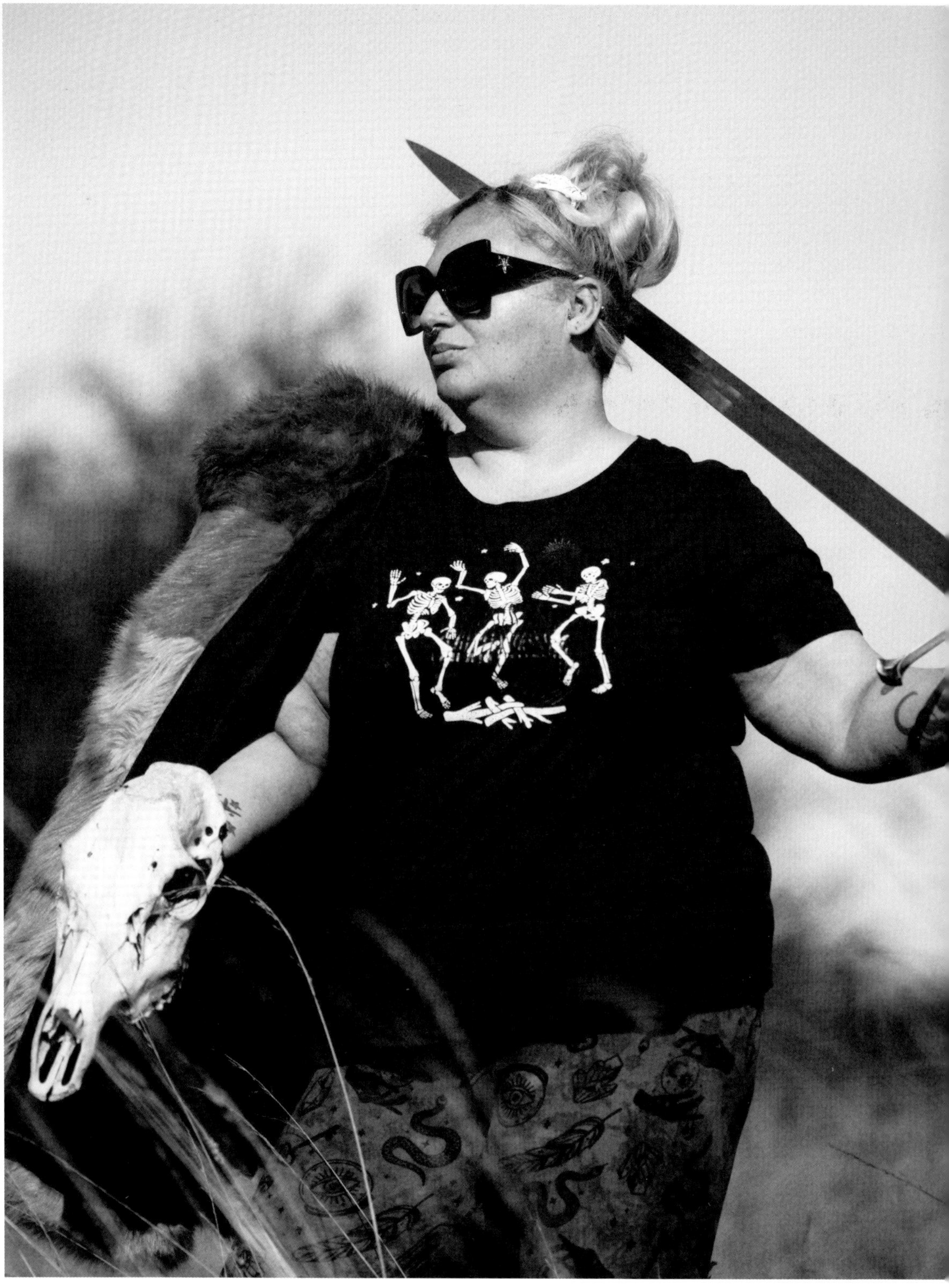

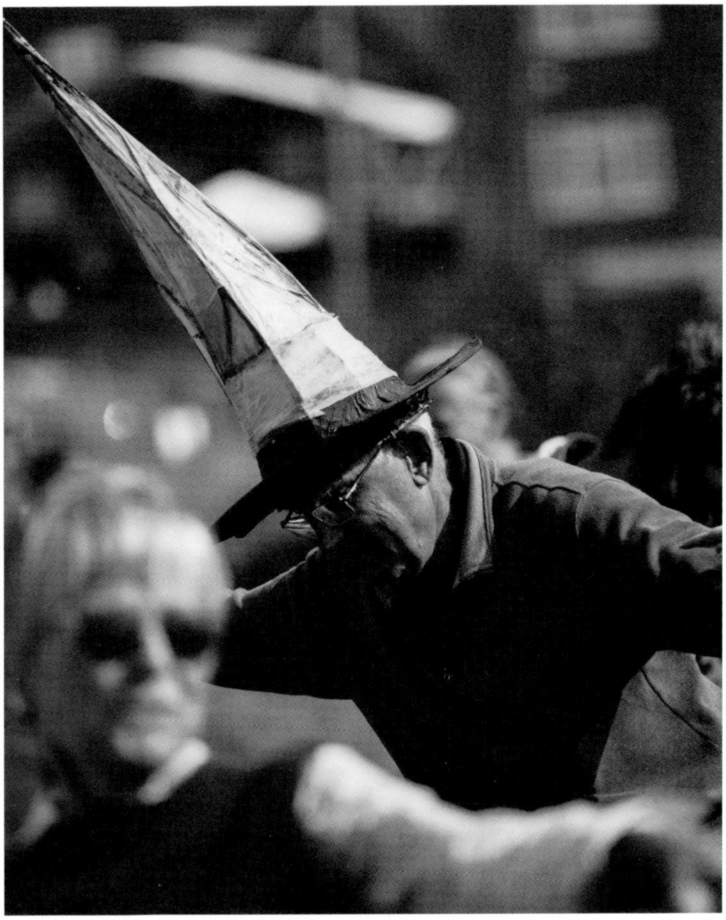

"A hyperactive village.
Punches above its weight.
Thinks it's a small town."

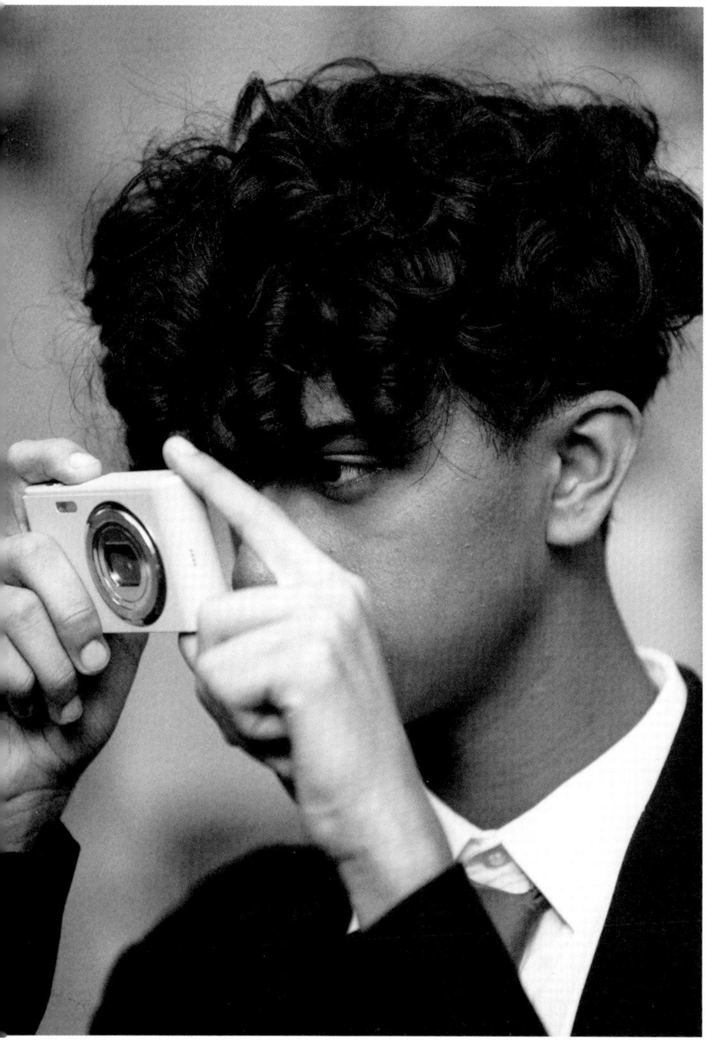

"2 pubs, the church,
2 shops, surgery, bus stop,
playing fields, scenic views
and many friends all in
walking distance."

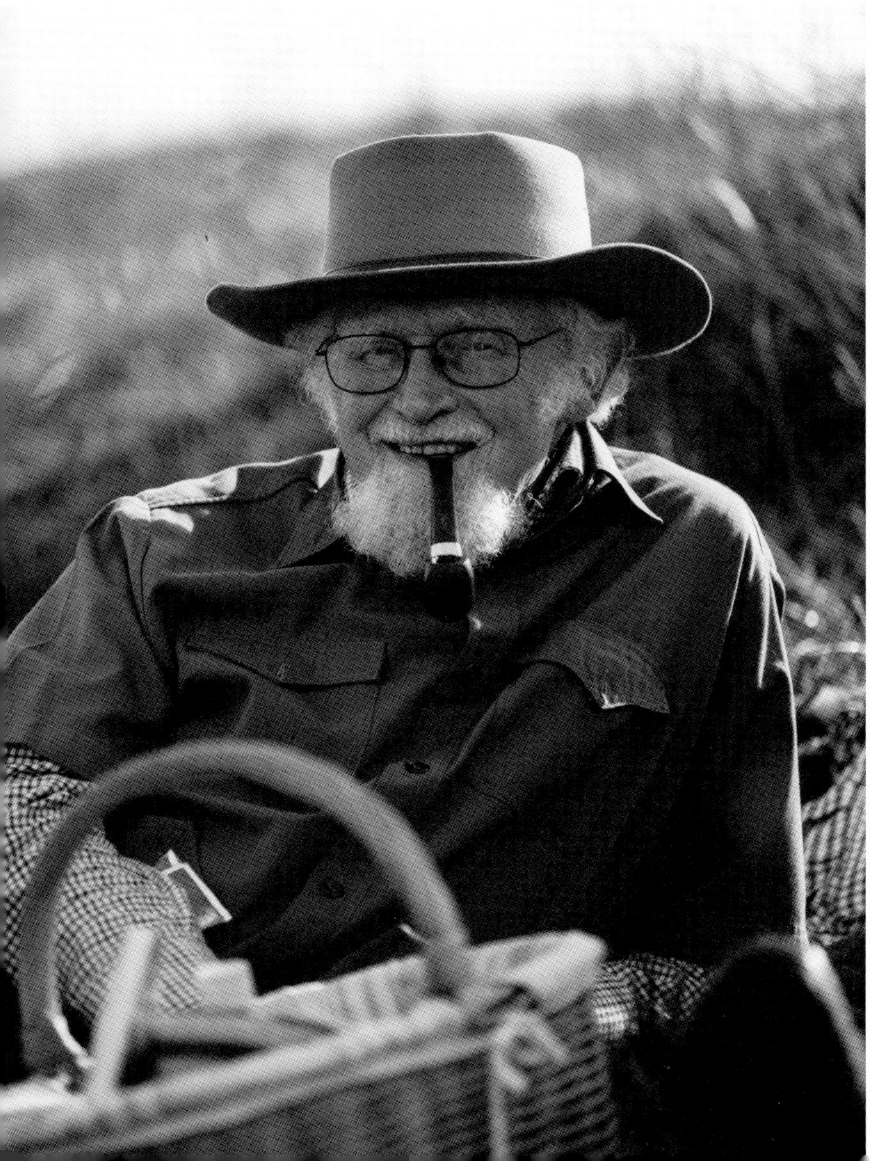

"I thought it had an unreal quality, almost as if it could be a movie set."

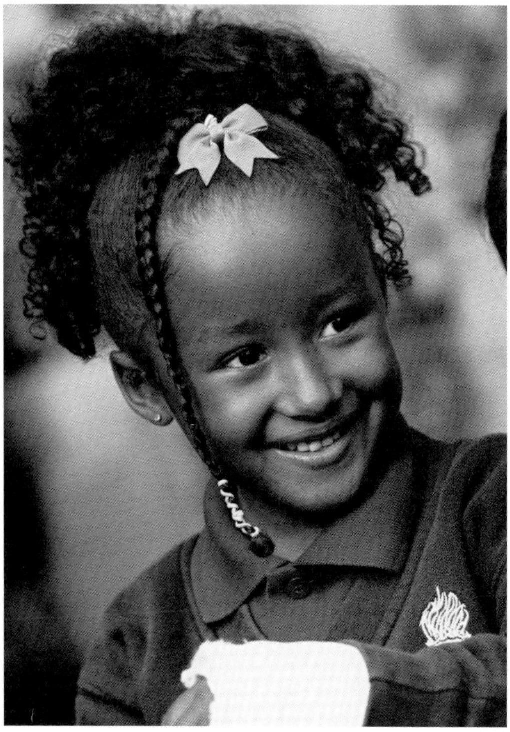

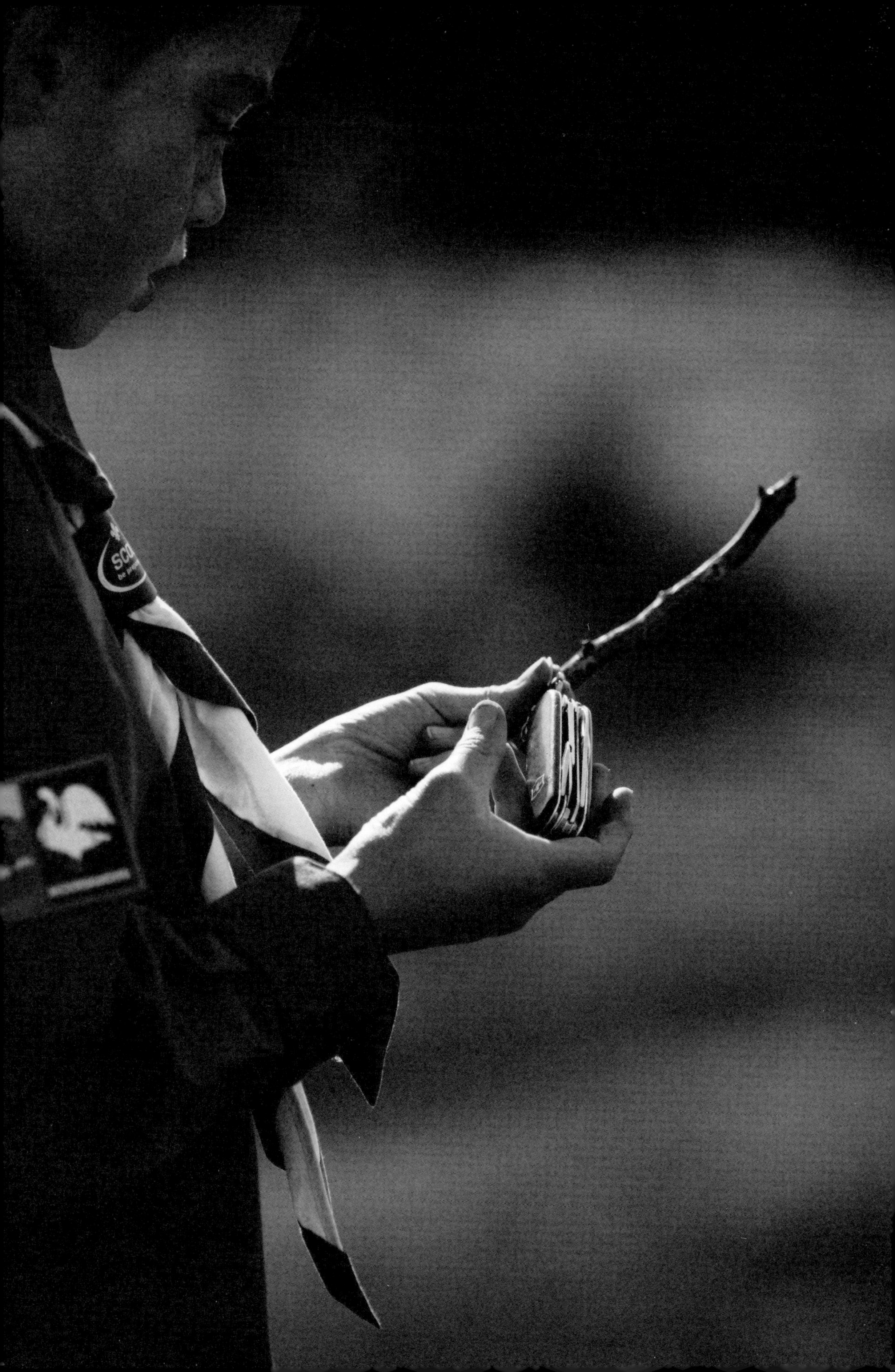

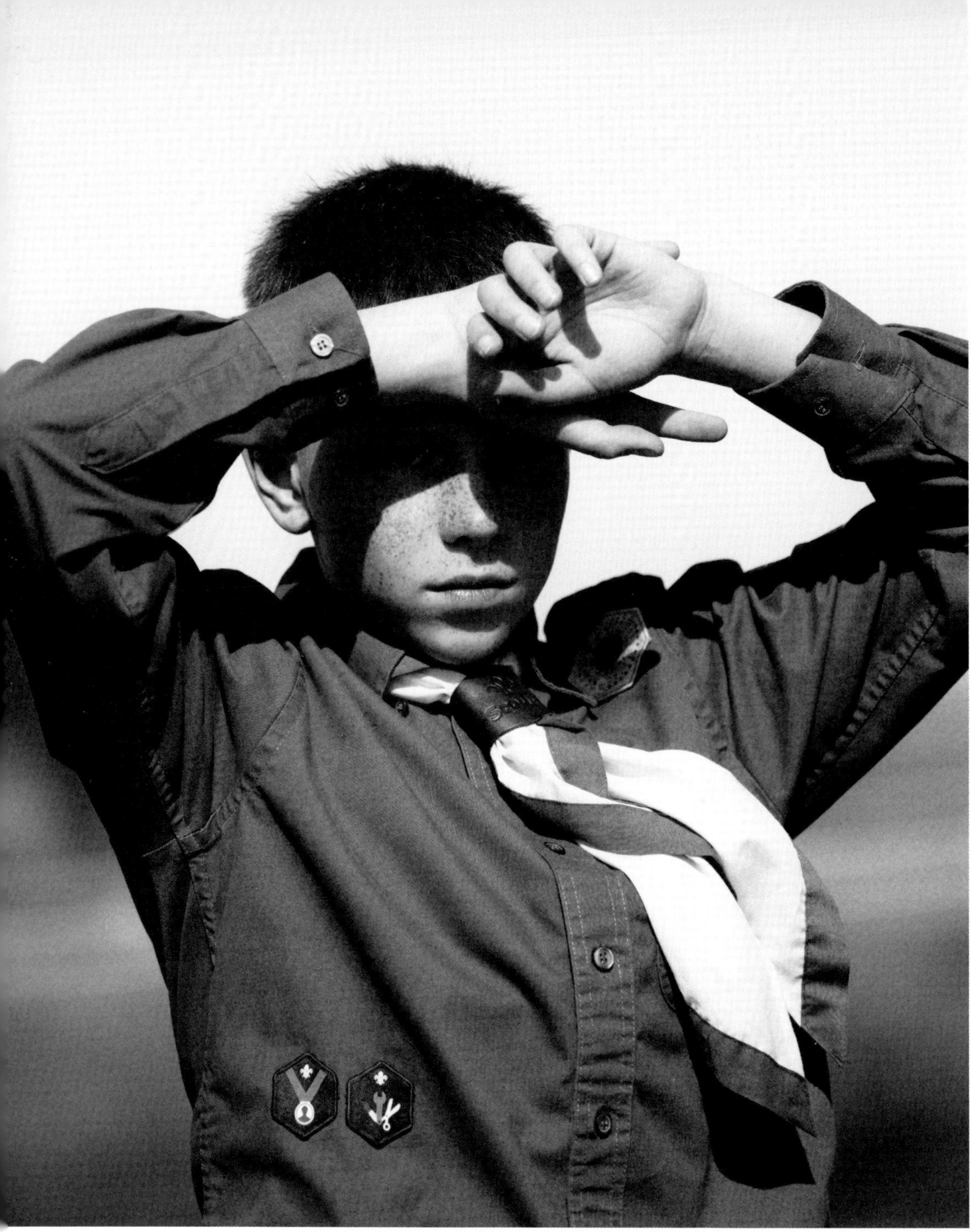

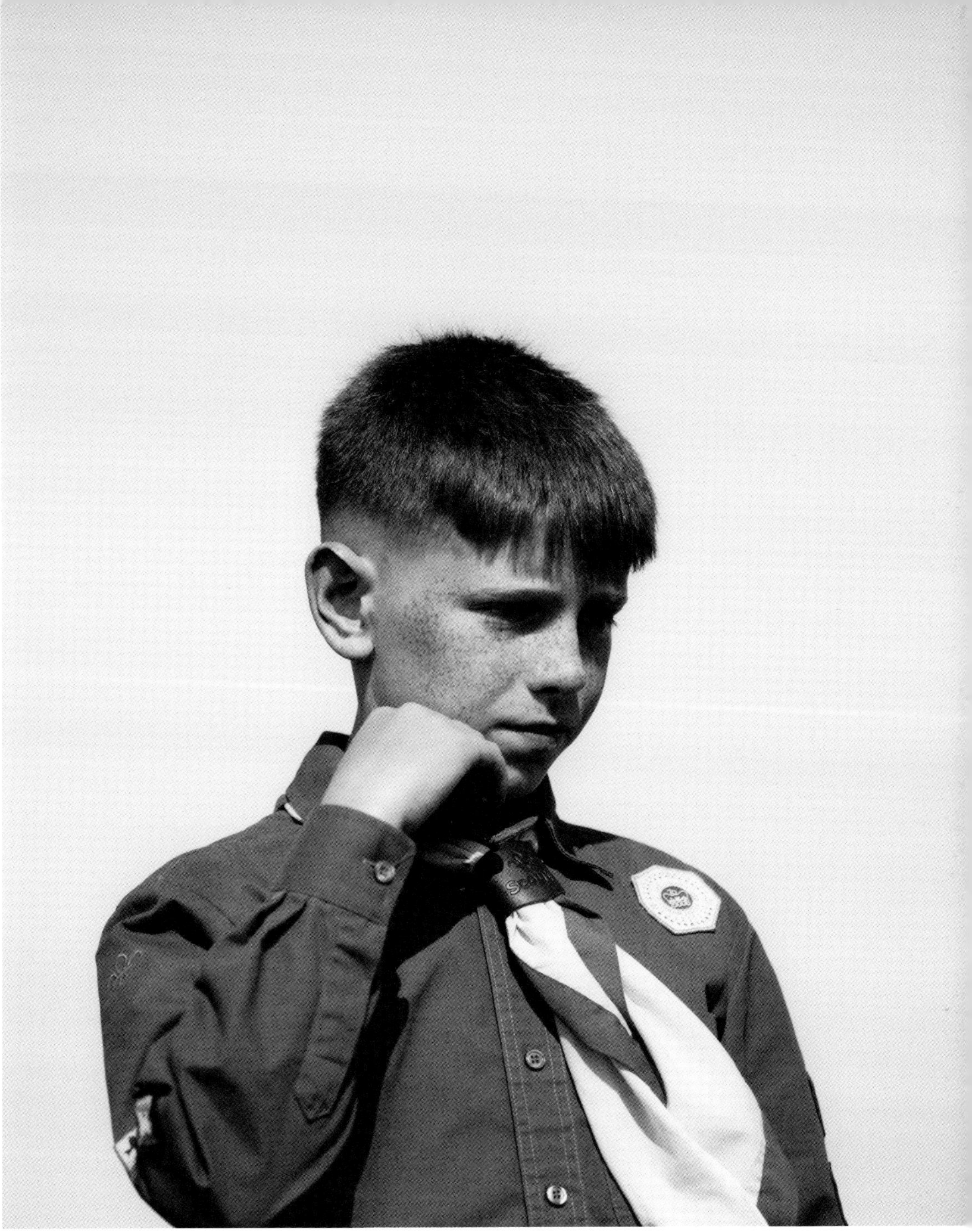

The village of

Fairford Leys

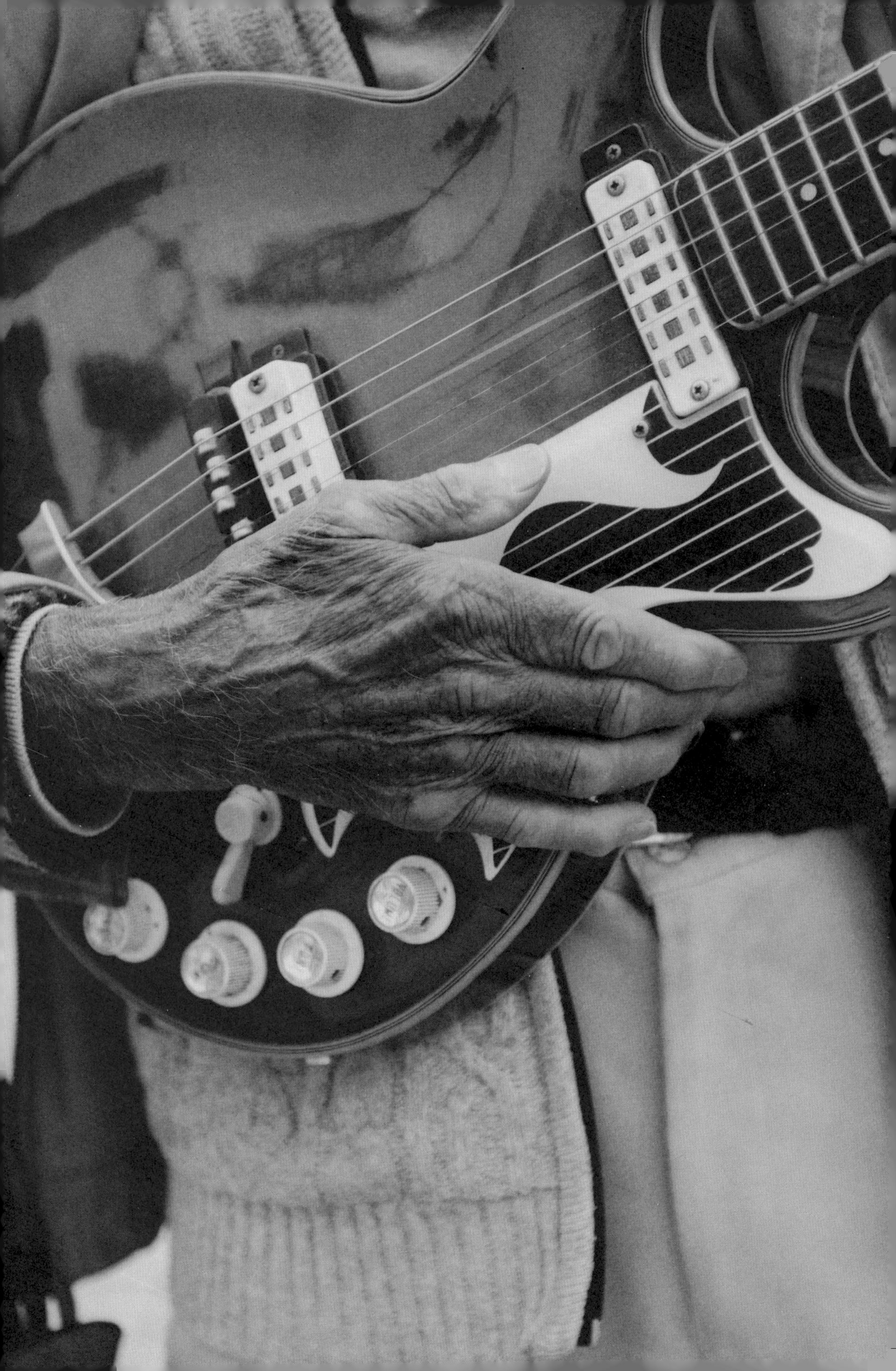

Fairford Leys

by
Will Burns

Late afternoon, late summer.
Late Victorian stylings—
railings, lamp posts, fog, sewage—
it was the year it never stopped raining.
But where was I again?
A mixed use development bound by green belt,
byroad *diverticula* and a 'design code'.
Brickwork. Austere brick church.
Strictly-regulated uniformly coloured doors
behind which vernacular lives run on specificity.
Local, distinct. A 'liveable community'—
an 'imaginative village' made out of imaginary villages.
The purpose built and the double (well-) meaninged—
Utopia (cafe), Bootcamp (gym), Brasserie (Chinese).
The starter homes and the houses which detach themselves
the further they get from the main square
and its traditional band stand.
The listed farmhouse at the centre of it all,
evidence of authentic old age, of rubber-stamped provenance.
The long-settled patch—farmstead, hamlet, outskirt.
That questionable 'Coldharbour' parish name
—hill, serpent, clearing? Camp, haven, shelter?
The Saxon, possibly satanic (so the old songs say) burial mounds,
the school grounds and shopmobility scooters.
Sunlit European lager on the metal table
outside the fish and chip shop.
The friendship group
and the mother and toddler group
and the church coffee morning group
and the book group and the golf group
and the five pints of Guinness in the Honey Bee group
(plus one today, watching cricket on the big screen).
Last orders? Jesus... time flies and all that.

"My home since 1981.
An exceptional community."

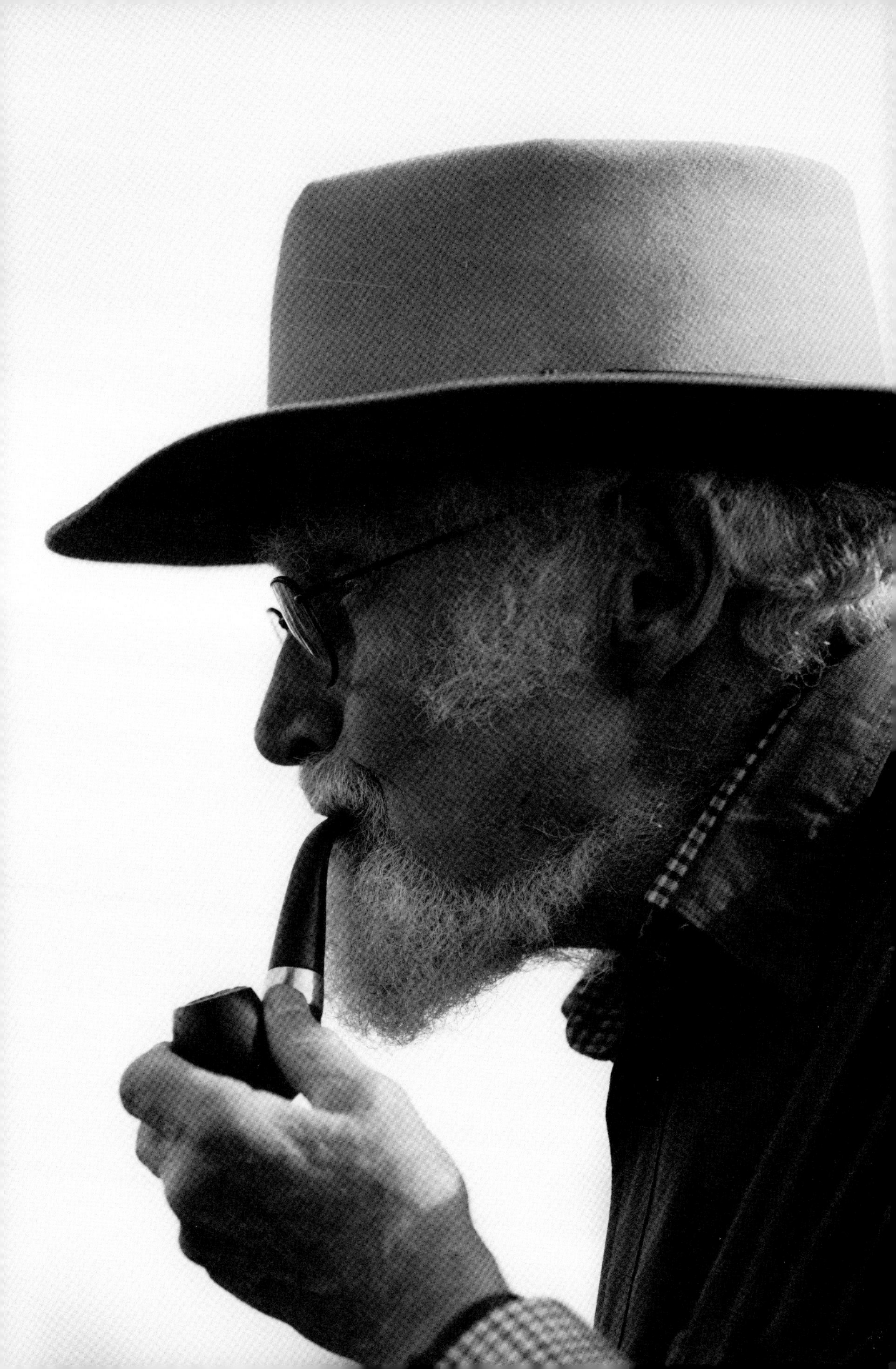

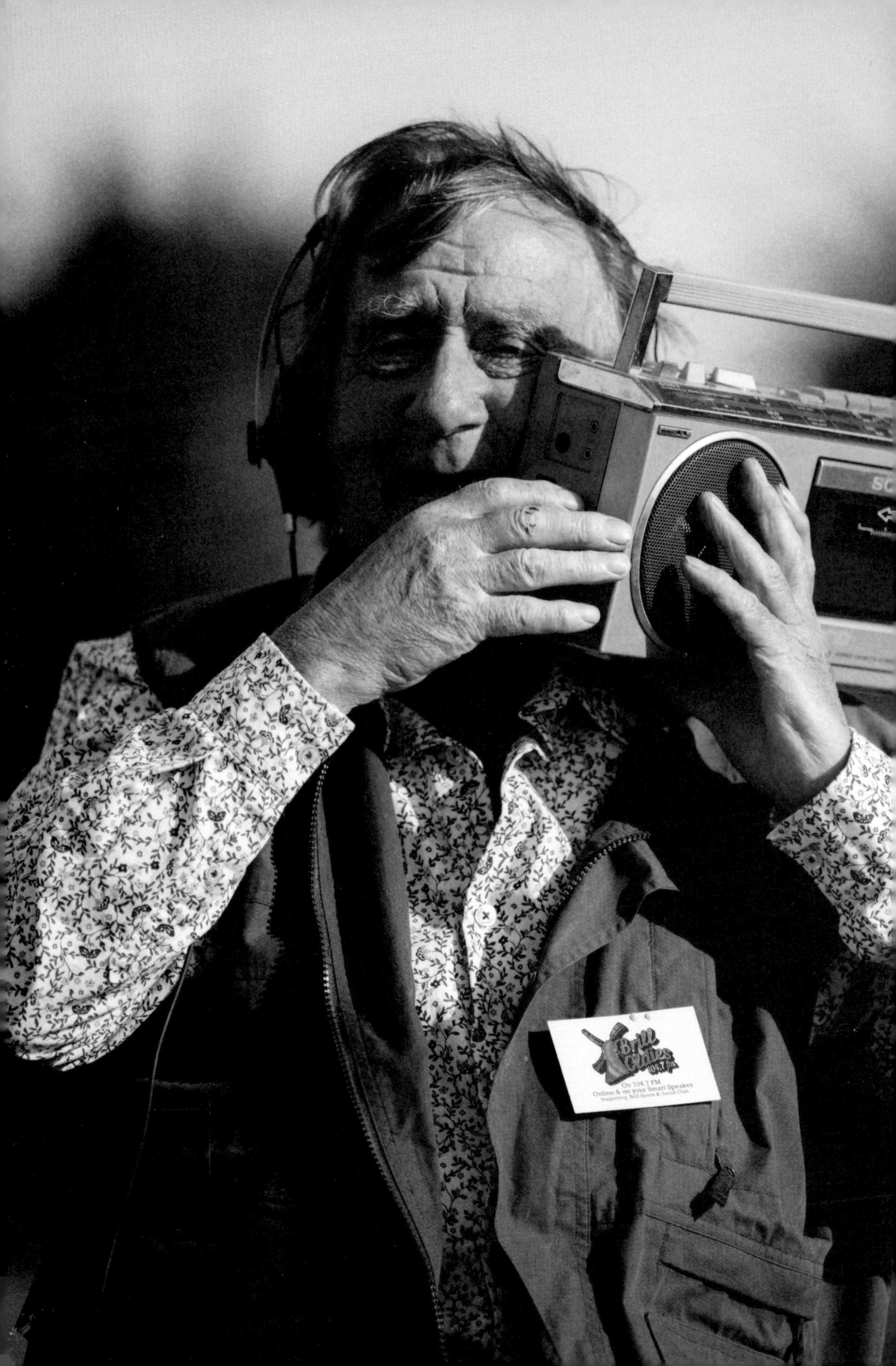
Brill Oldies 104.7 fm
On 104.7 FM
Online & on your Smart Speaker
Supporting Brill Sports & Social Club

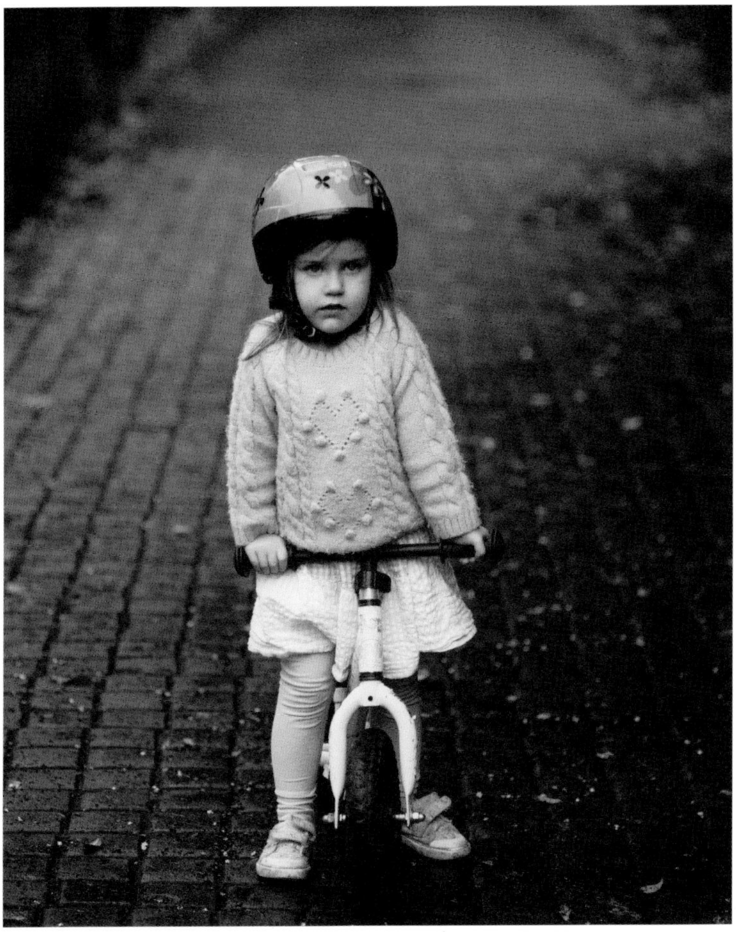

"It is everything you want a community to be. I walk to the shops and always see someone I know."

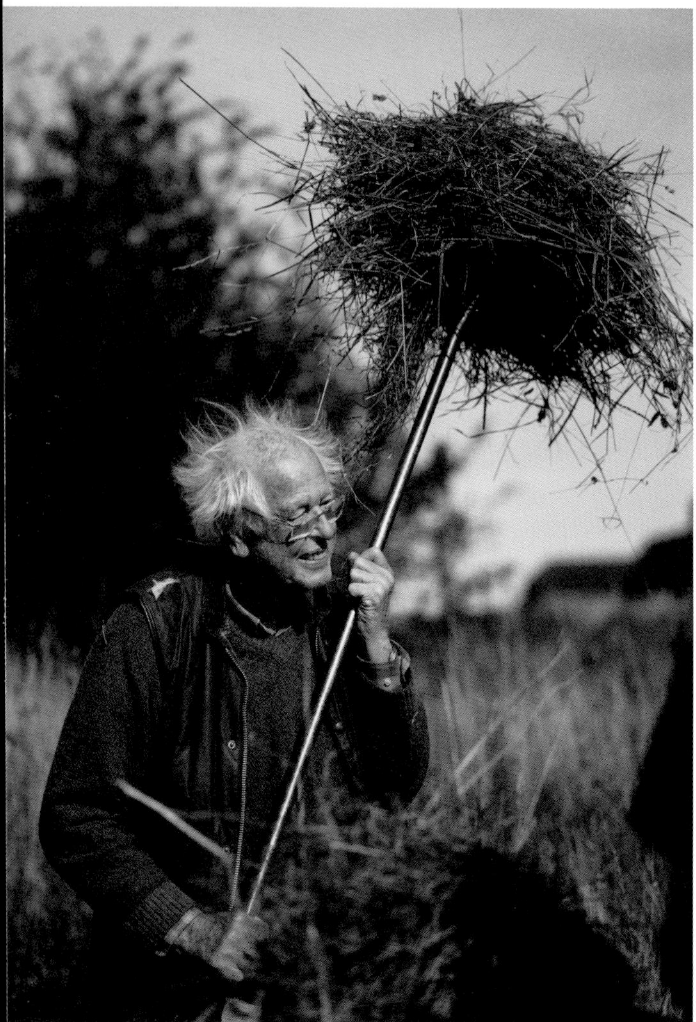

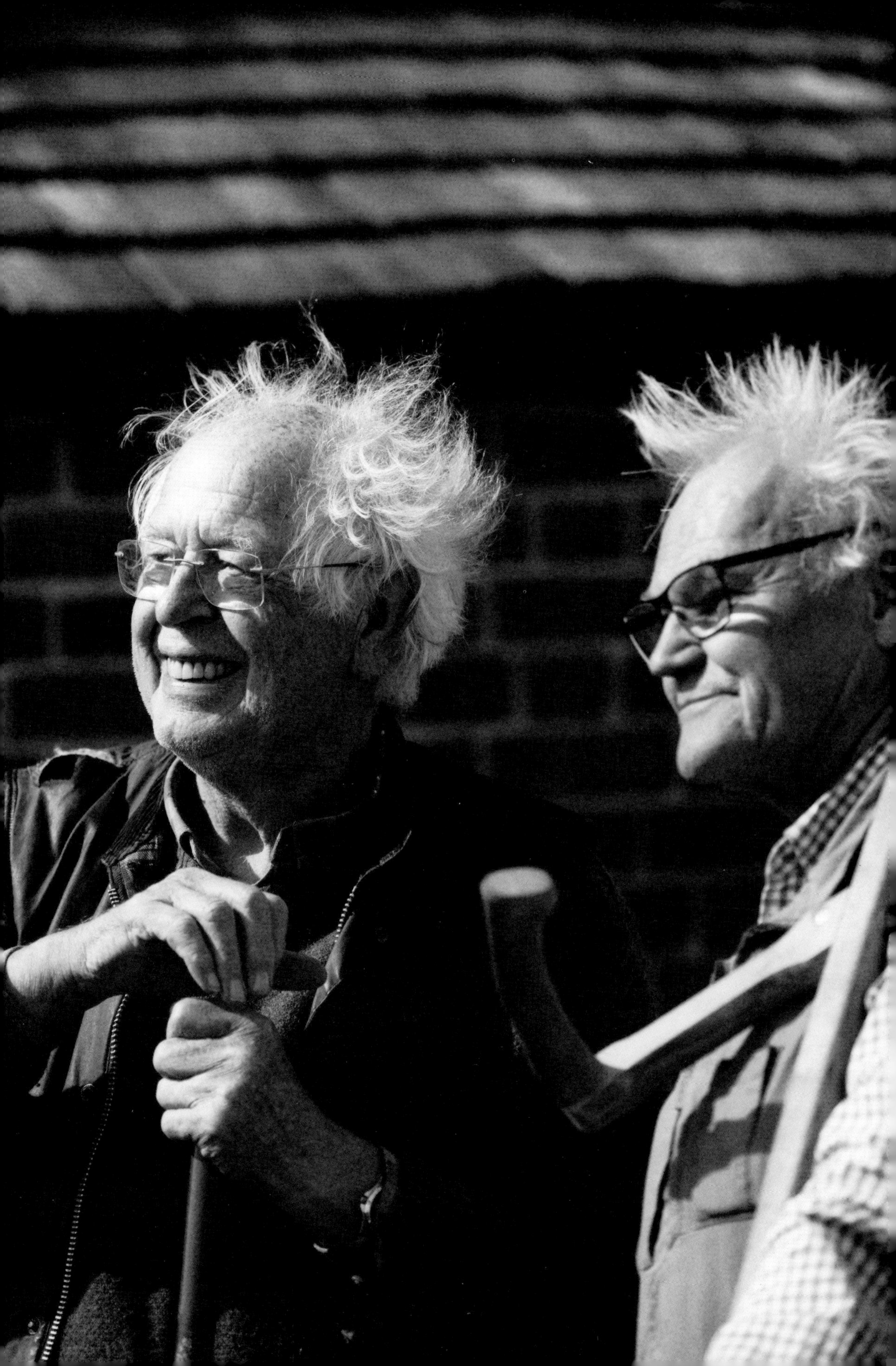

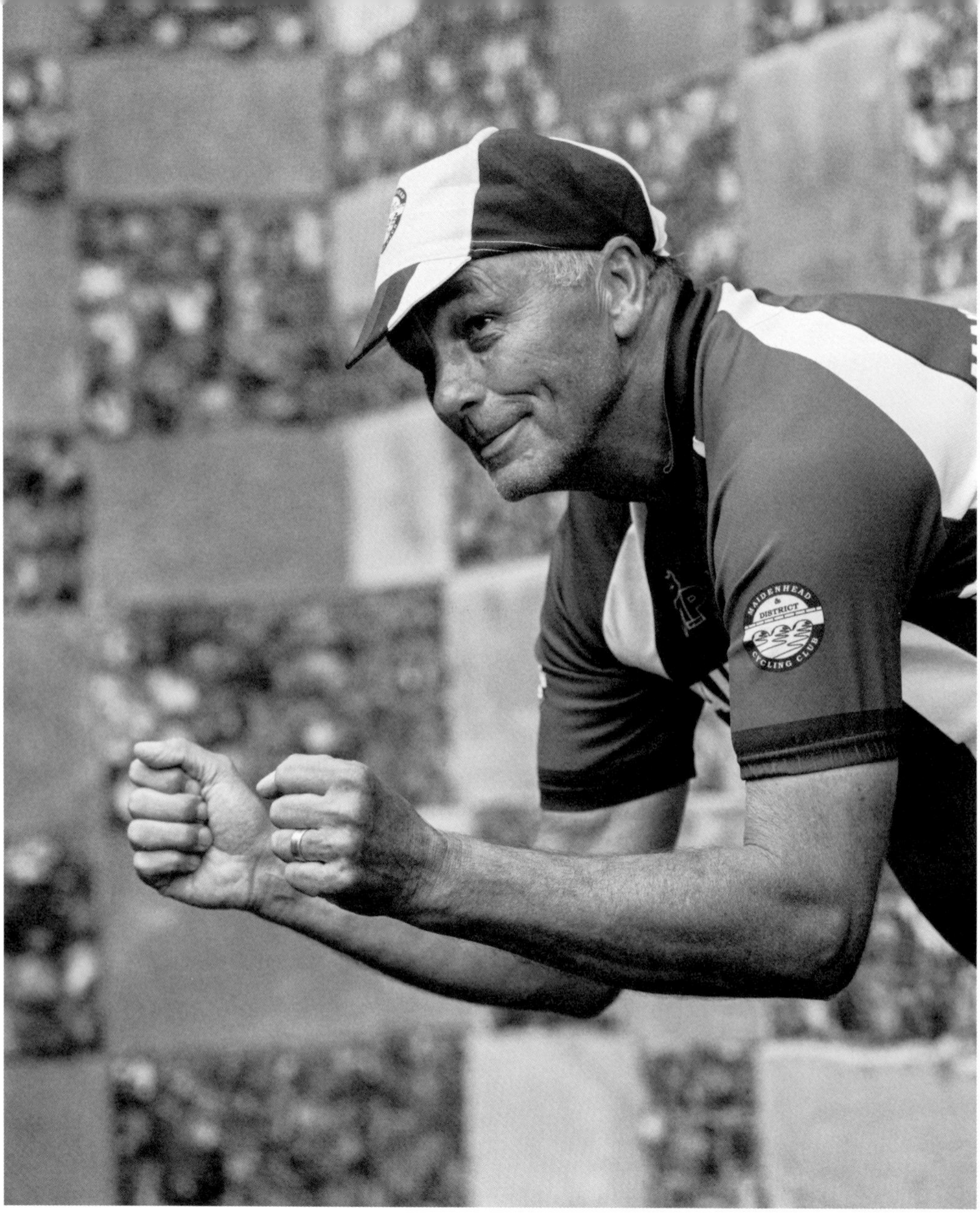
MAIDENHEAD
&
DISTRICT
CYCLING CLUB

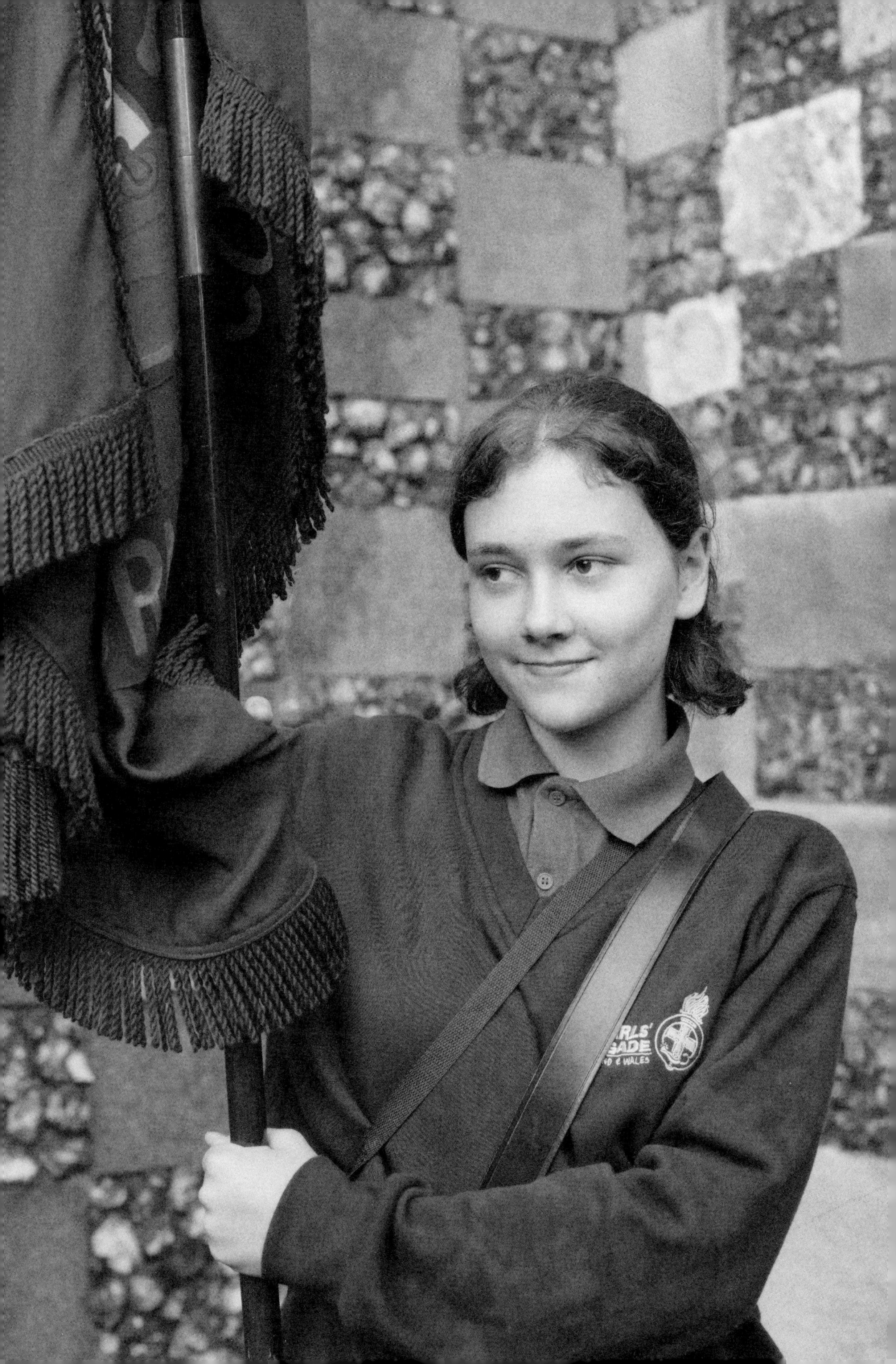

*"A place of history.
An island surrounded by the
madness of the modern."*

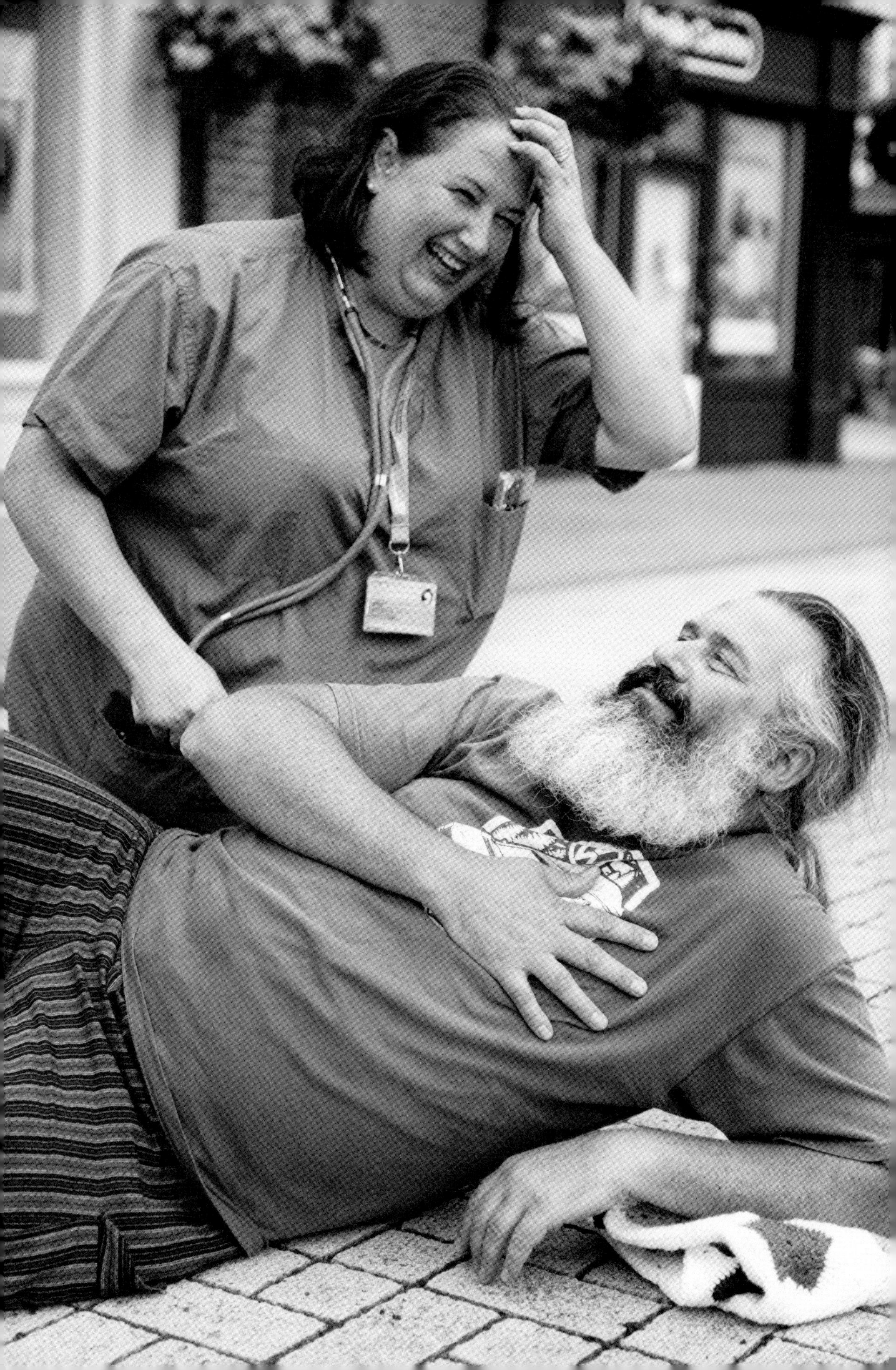

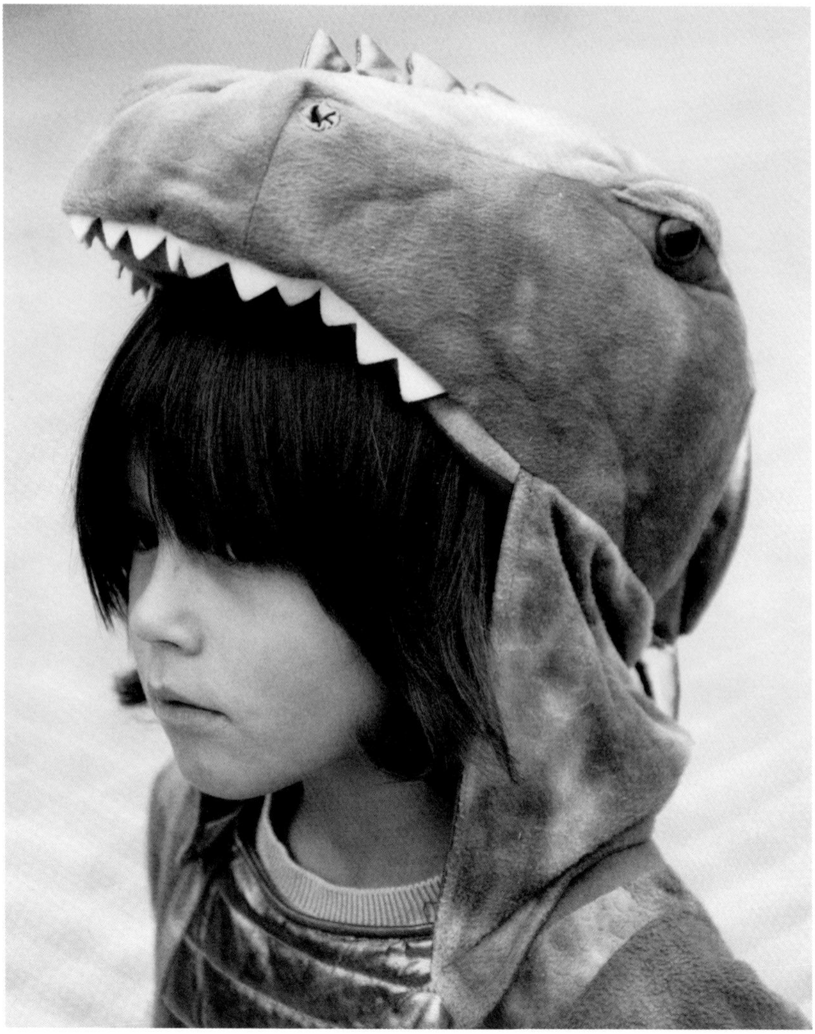

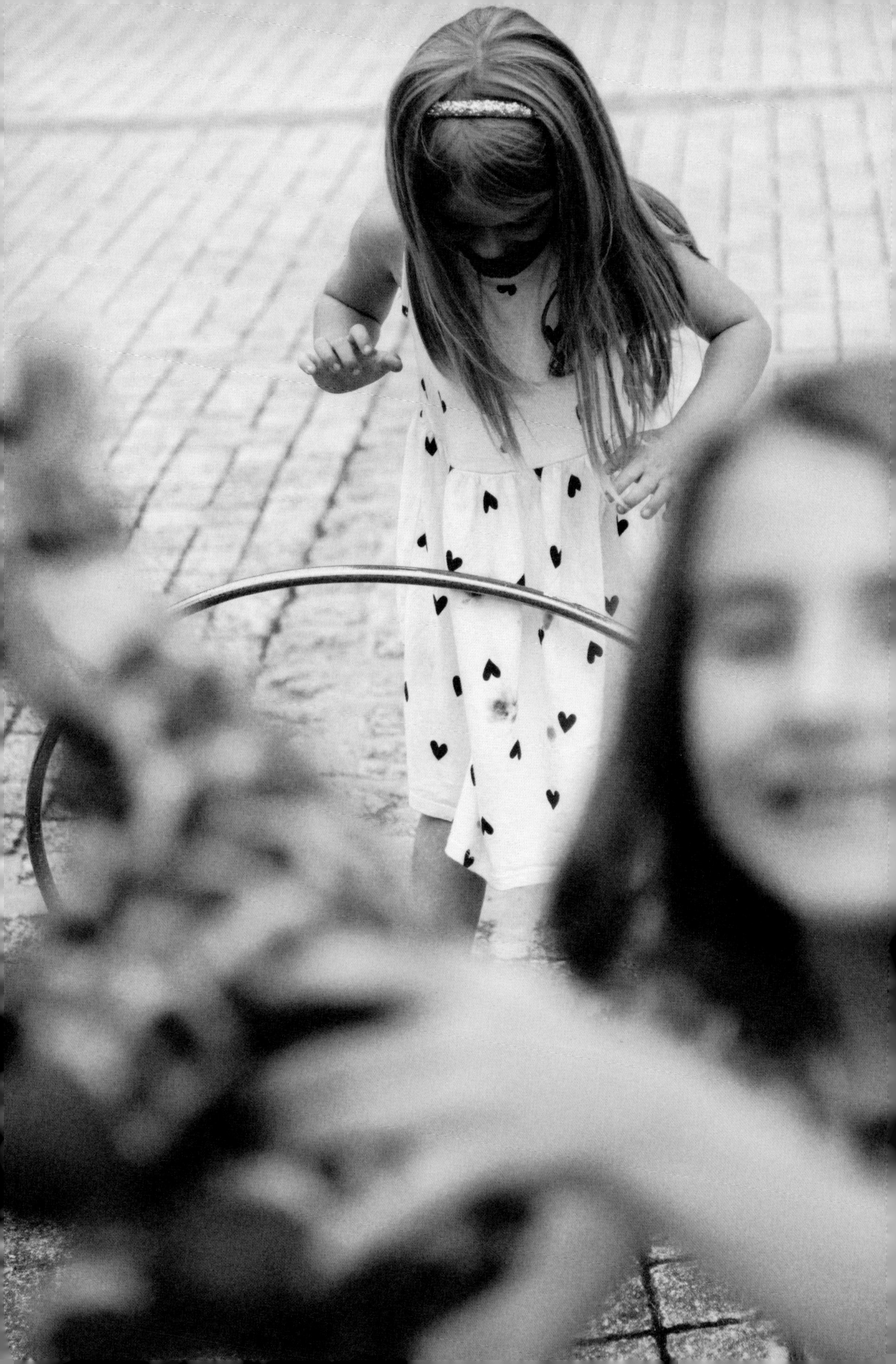

The

village

of

Burnham

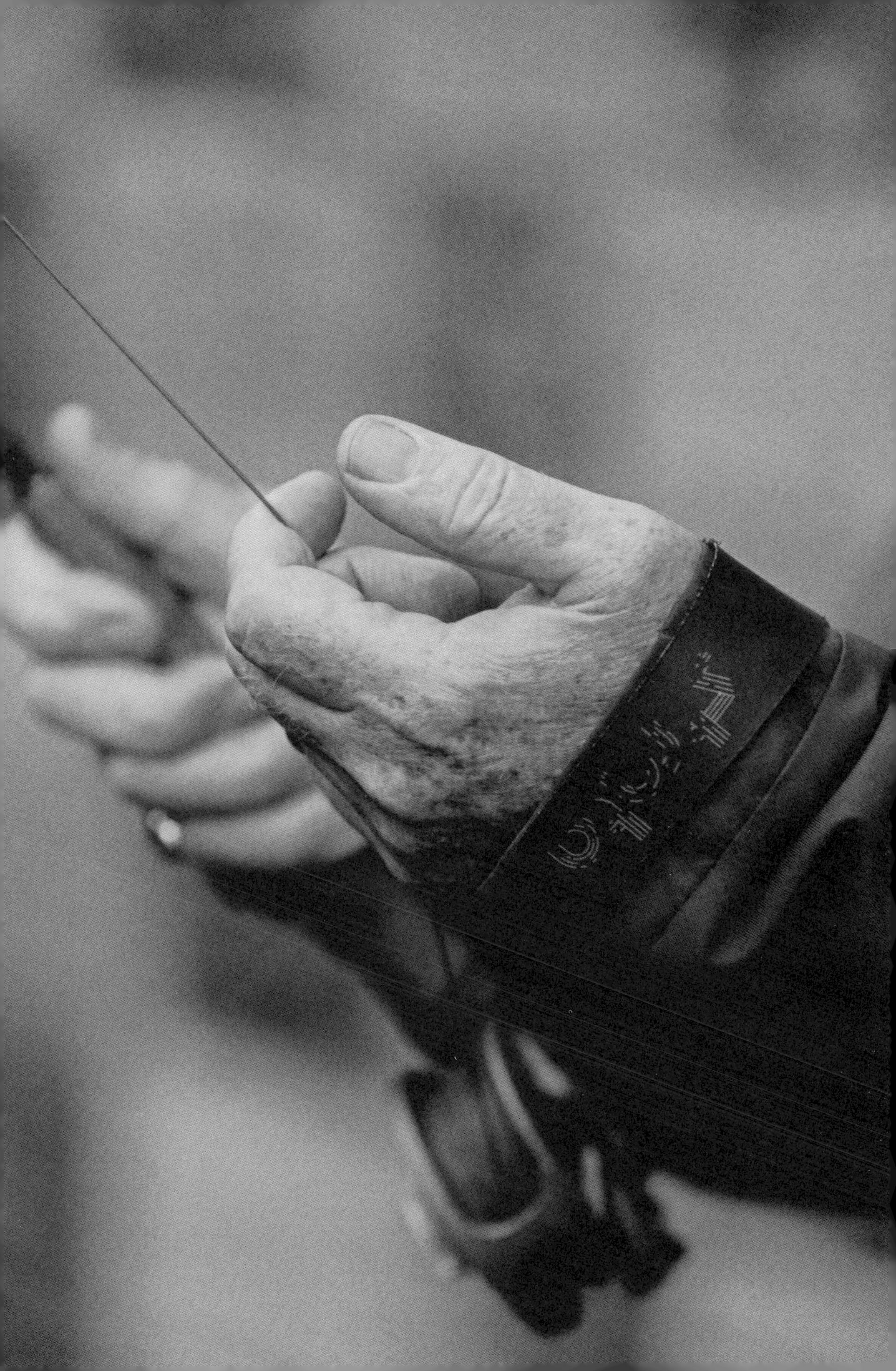

Hand in Hand

by Claire Fuller

Greg Timmins, litter picker extraordinaire (as he calls himself) finds a severed hand in the bin outside Tesco Express. This bin has often proved fruitful: an open packet of tan tights (a gift for long-time girlfriend, Julie—unappreciated), an unopened turkey sandwich (eaten by his good self—a bit dry), and a pair of New Balance trainers (saved for the boy, whenever he makes the effort to come and see his old dad). But a severed hand is a first.

He would hand it in (get it?) to the coppers, except that on one finger a diamond ring glitters, and Julie has been angling for an engagement for three years. Greg pulls at the ring, but it won't come off.

At home, he soaps the hand (chilly but surprisingly soft), pours on washing-up liquid, tries the ribbon trick the Internet suggests. The ring will not budge. He places the hand on a chopping board, gets his sharpest knife (not very sharp to tell the truth) but cannot bring himself to cut. The hand (he sees now) has small delicate fingers, the nails painted duck-egg blue. He lays it in an empty cigar box (from the same bin) and leaves it on the table next to the magazine article about Caribbean honeymoons which Julie has left open.

When she comes round that evening she complains about a bad smell and says she isn't prepared to stay in such a stink. Greg can't smell anything, and after she's gone, he takes out the hand, cradling it and then intertwining their fingers. (Laughing, he gives it a name: Lucy). He kisses Lucy's palm, and tenderly she strokes his face. That night Lucy sleeps on the pillow where Julie's head sometimes lies.

Two weeks later Greg sends out the invitations to the engagement party.

Can't Help Falling in Love

by Claire Fuller

As Brian steps in front of the mic, one of his sideburns begins to slip down his cheek – the stage light is too bright and too hot and has melted the glue. Ignoring it, he opens with *Viva La Vegas*, loud and showy, remembering his ex-wife who'd loved him when his sideburns and quiff were his own; before she left him for a man who'd won big on the lottery. He follows this with *A Little Less Conversation*, in the hope that the clientele of the Burnham Curry House will stop talking and listen.

It's hard to see past the stage light's dazzle but he can tell the place is only half full – a couple of hen nights, the brides-to-be already drunk when Brian begins *Heartbreak Hotel*. He thinks of his cold and lonely bedsit, as a piece of naan bread flies past his ear. Something is wrong with his amp, and it will only work if he keeps one blue suede shoe pressed on the cable which connects it to the jack. It means he's limited to a wide-legged stance and a knee twitch, and can't do the full hip gyrations which is bound to result in less cash in the hat, although it's better news for his sciatica. He ends the first half with *Crying in the Chapel* and goes out the back for a fag.

When he returns, he curls his top lip and sings *His Latest Flame*. There isn't any applause. After a couple more numbers he sends around the hat, unplugs his guitar, and sings softly, *Are you Lonesome Tonight?* When the hat returns it contains two pounds and three pence, and a note. He unfolds it. Someone has replied: *Yes*. Brian's other sideburn begins to slip as he shades his eyes against the glare.

*"It was a small and friendly village.
But has sadly grown over the years and
nearly been absorbed."*

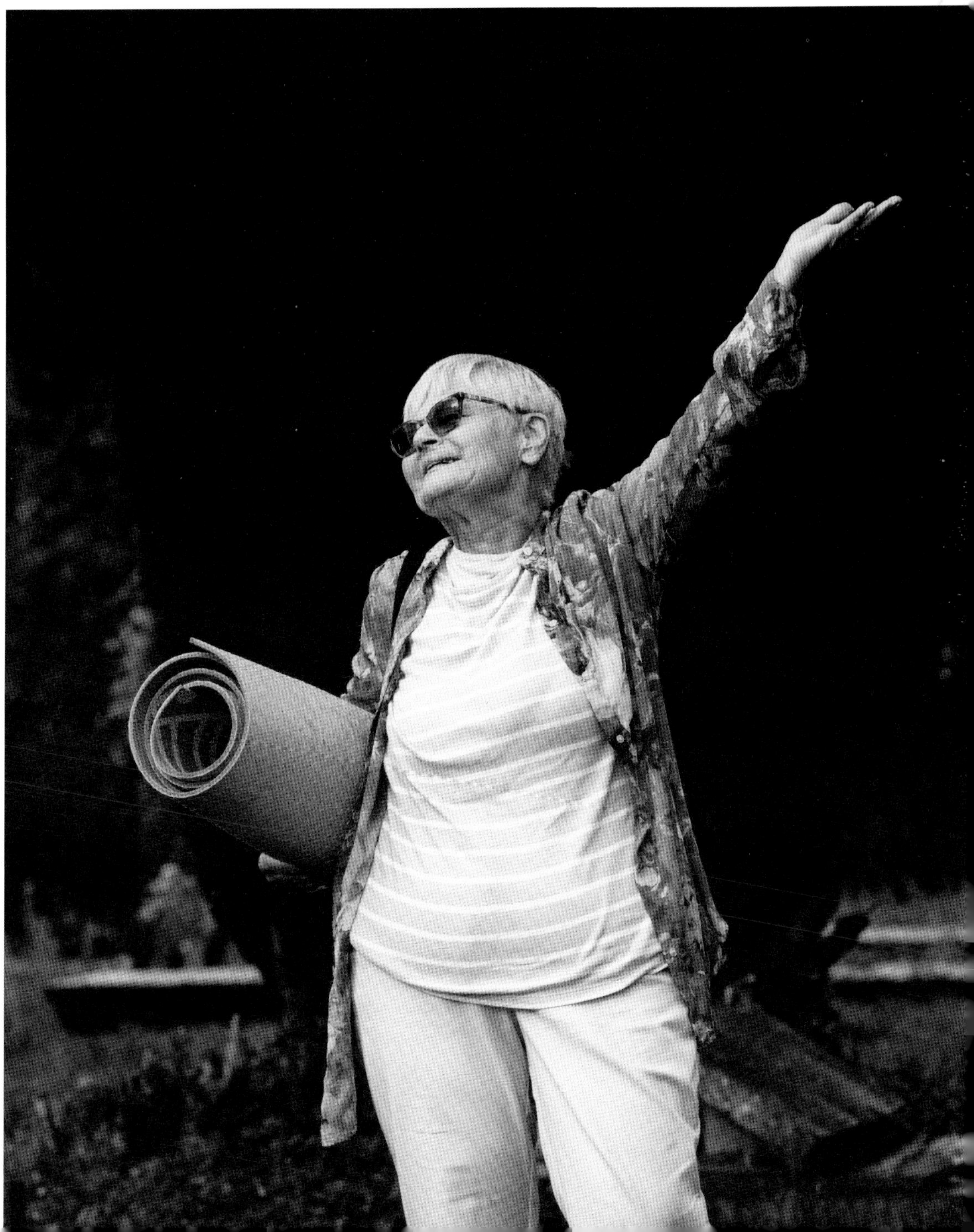

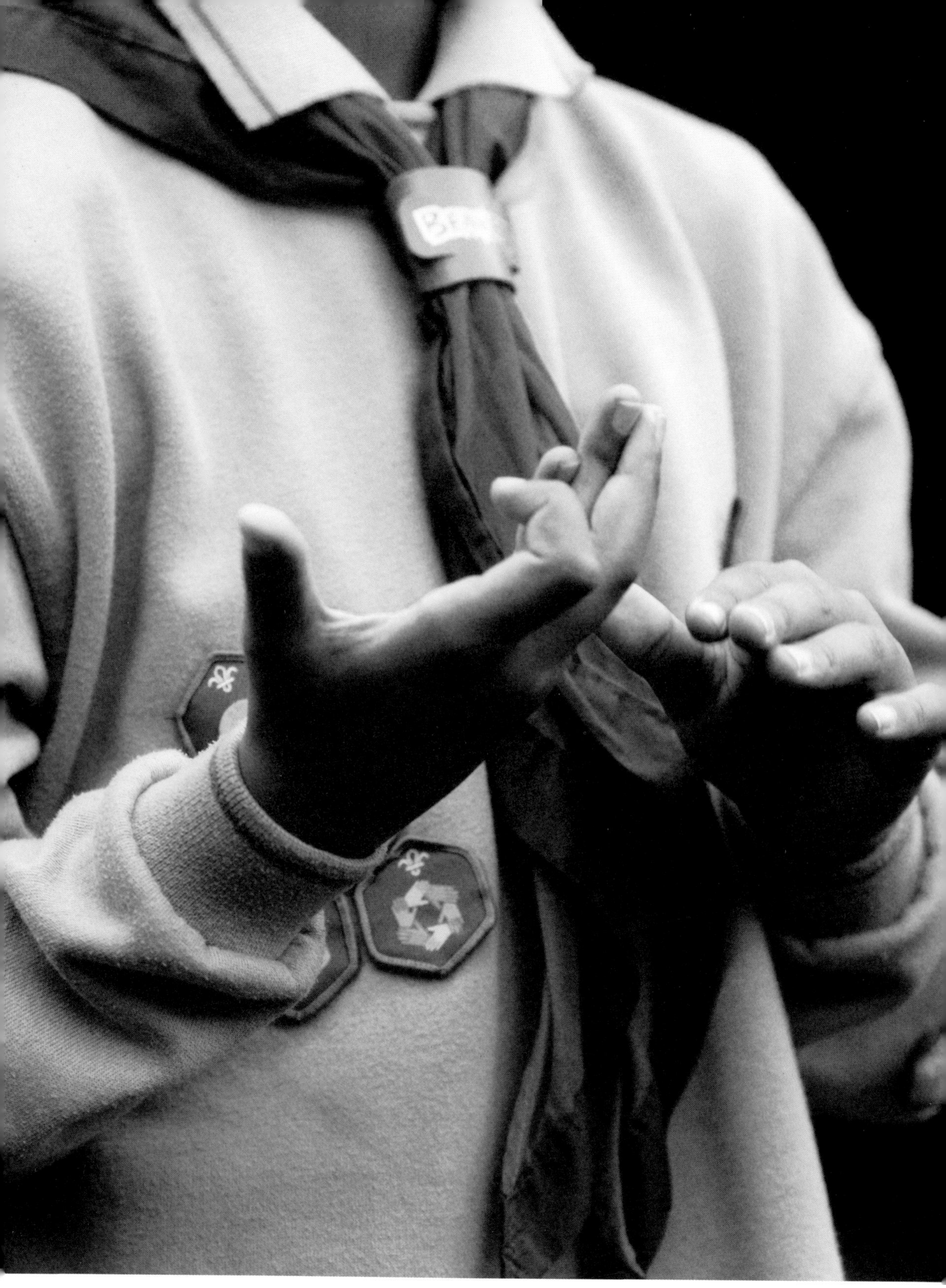

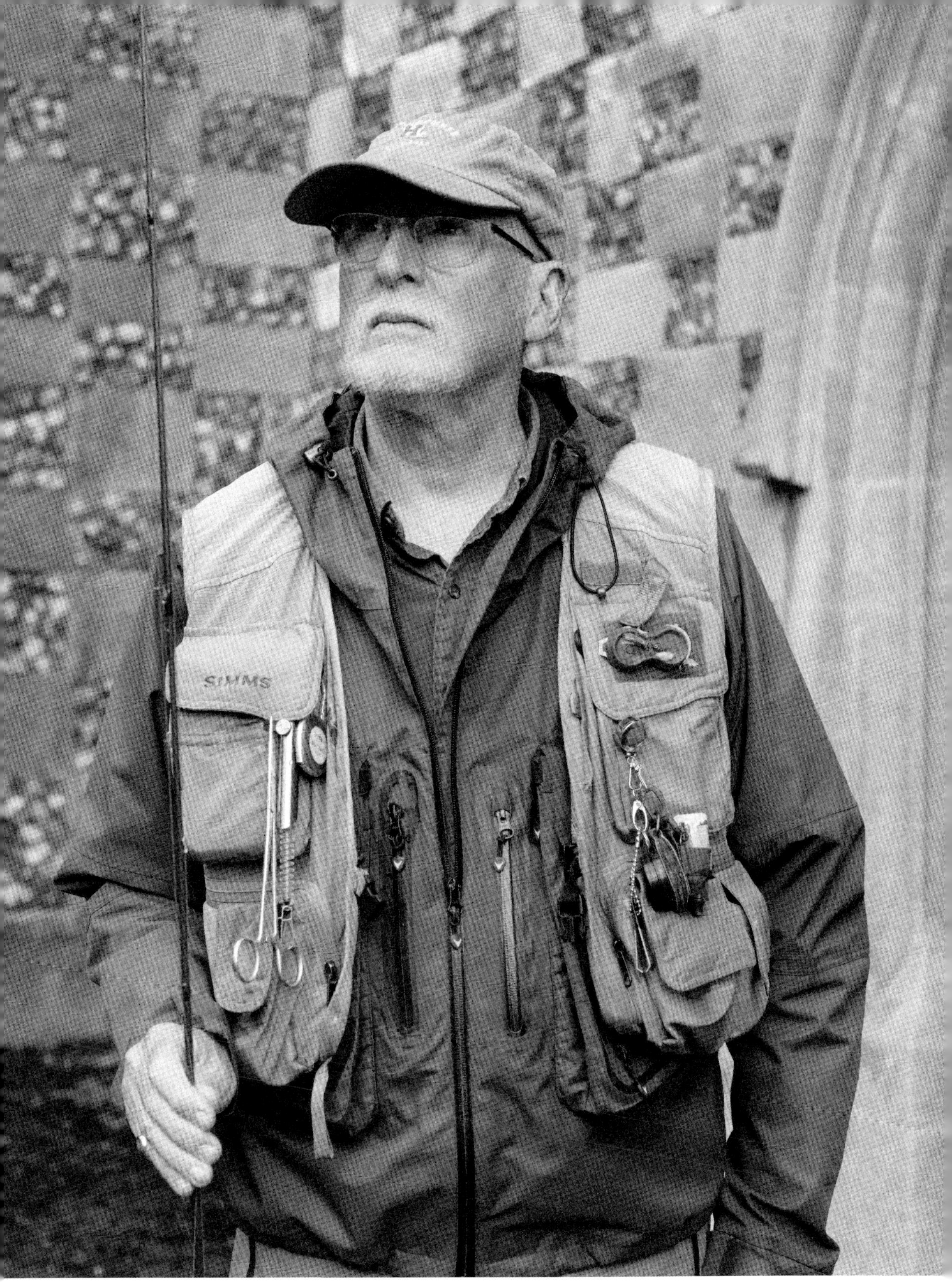
SIMMS

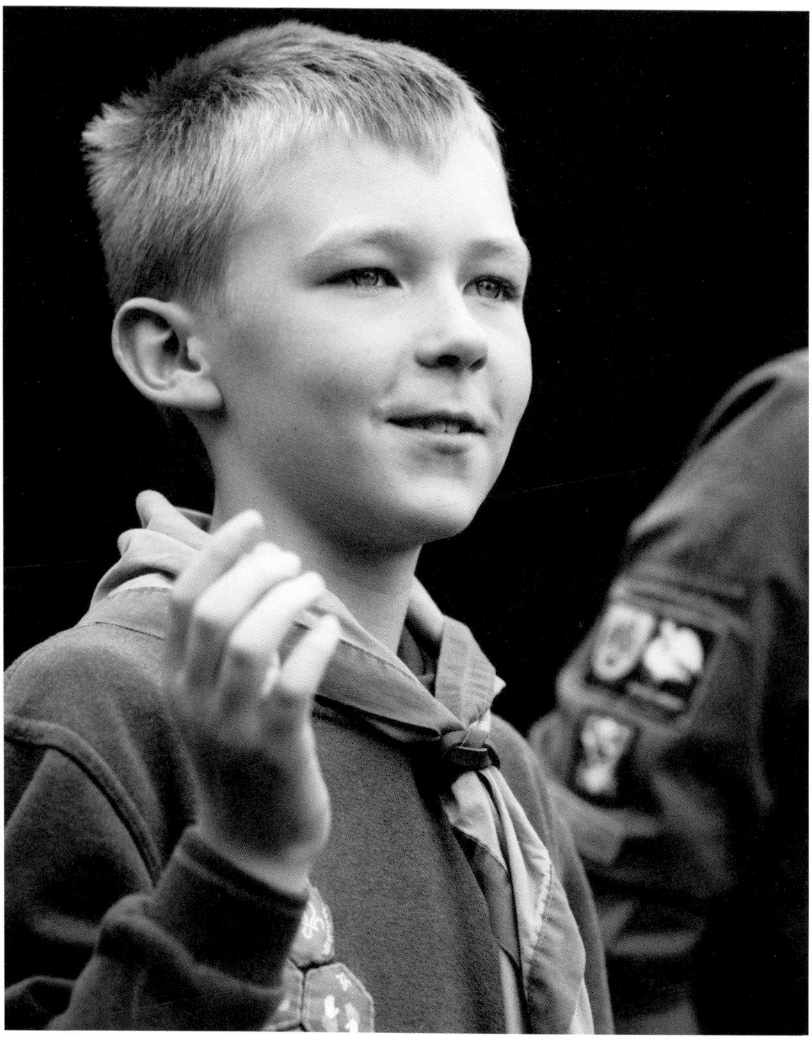

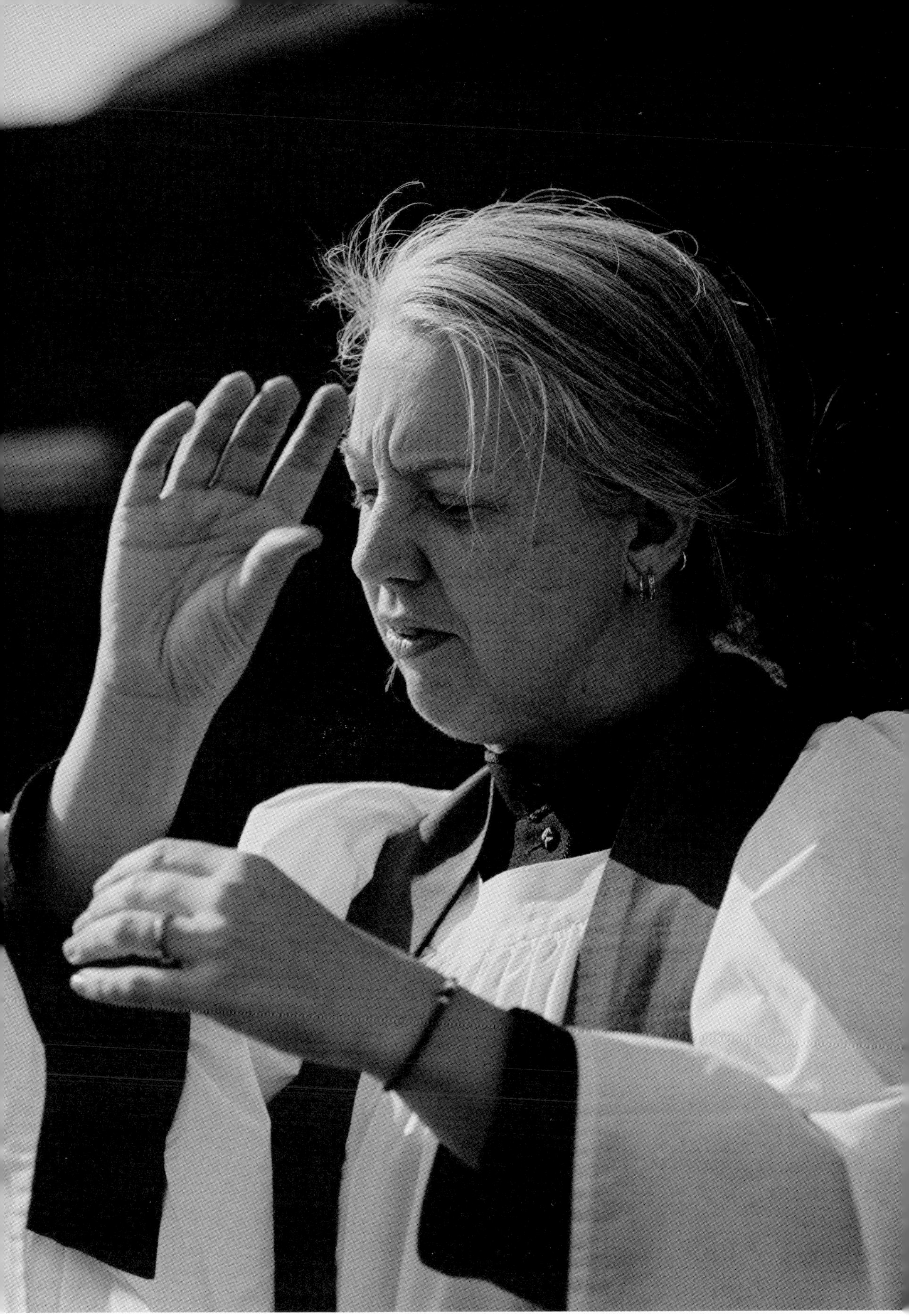

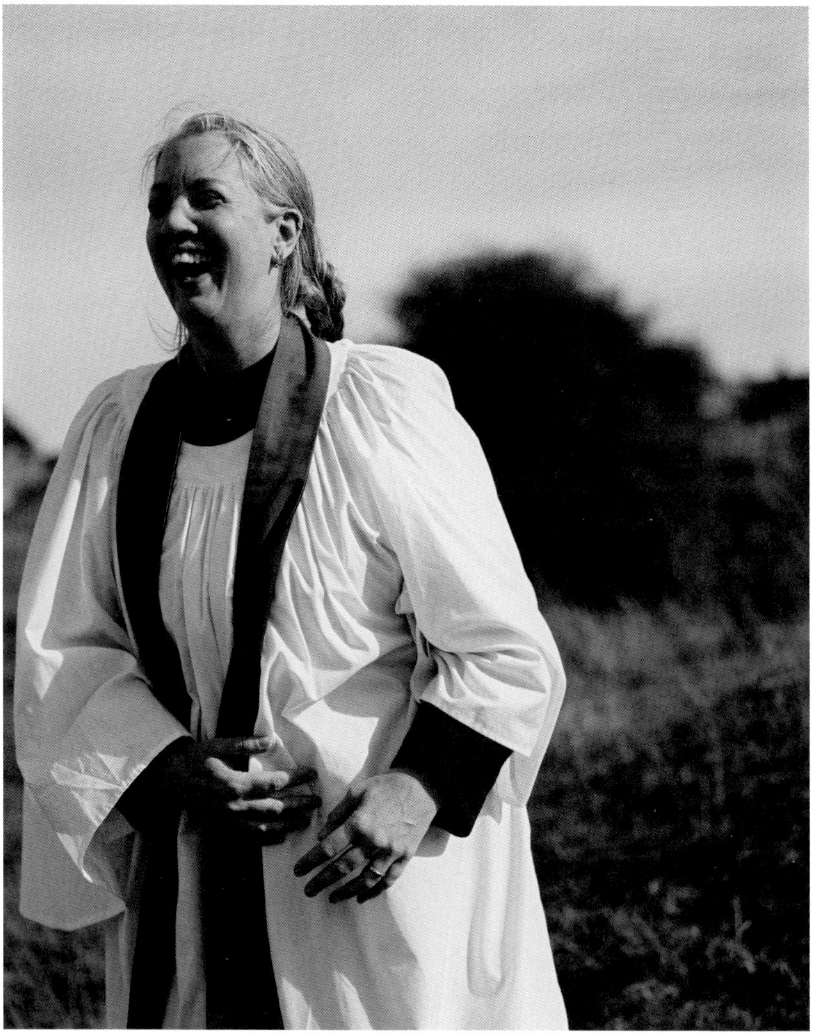

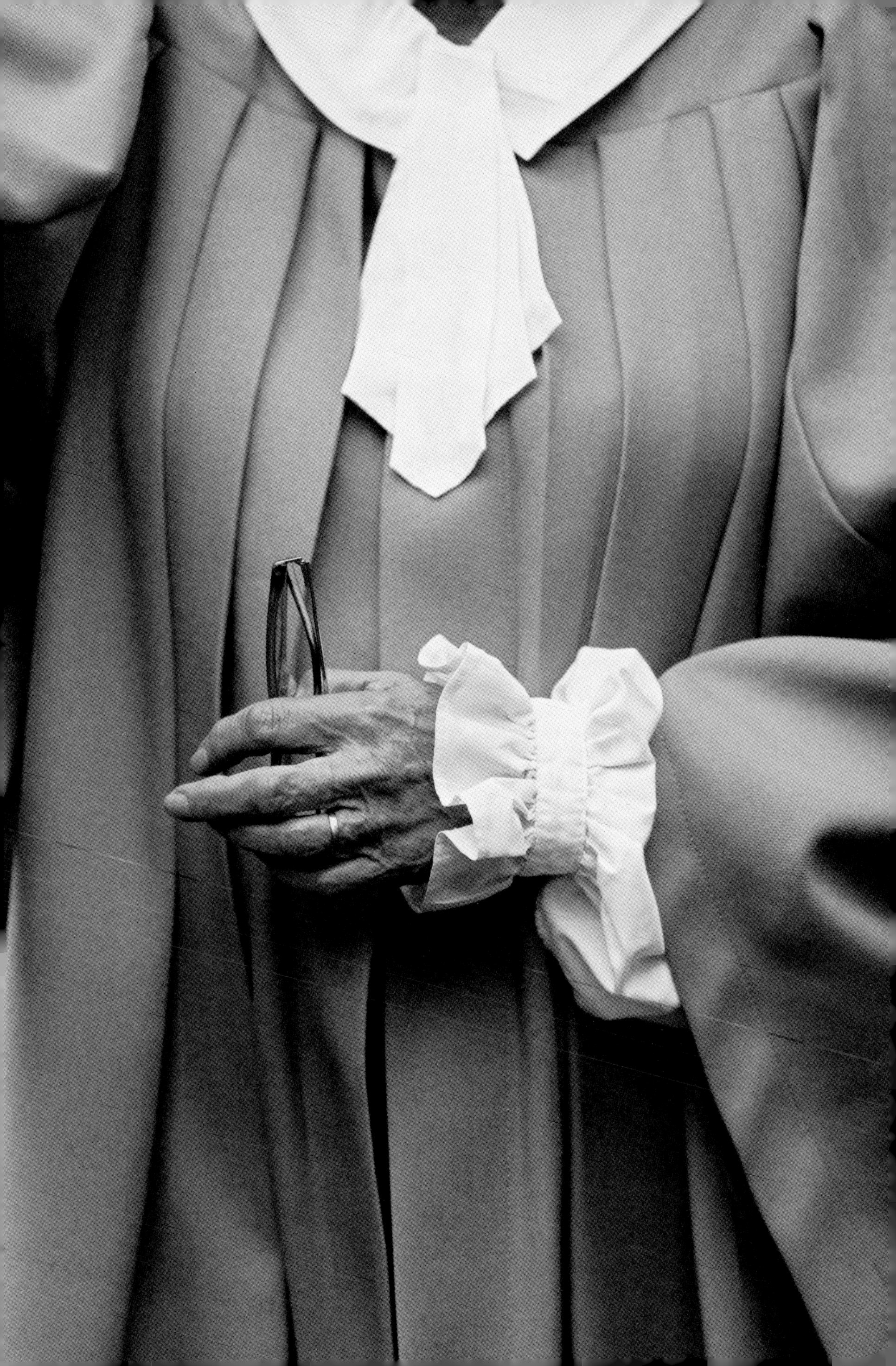

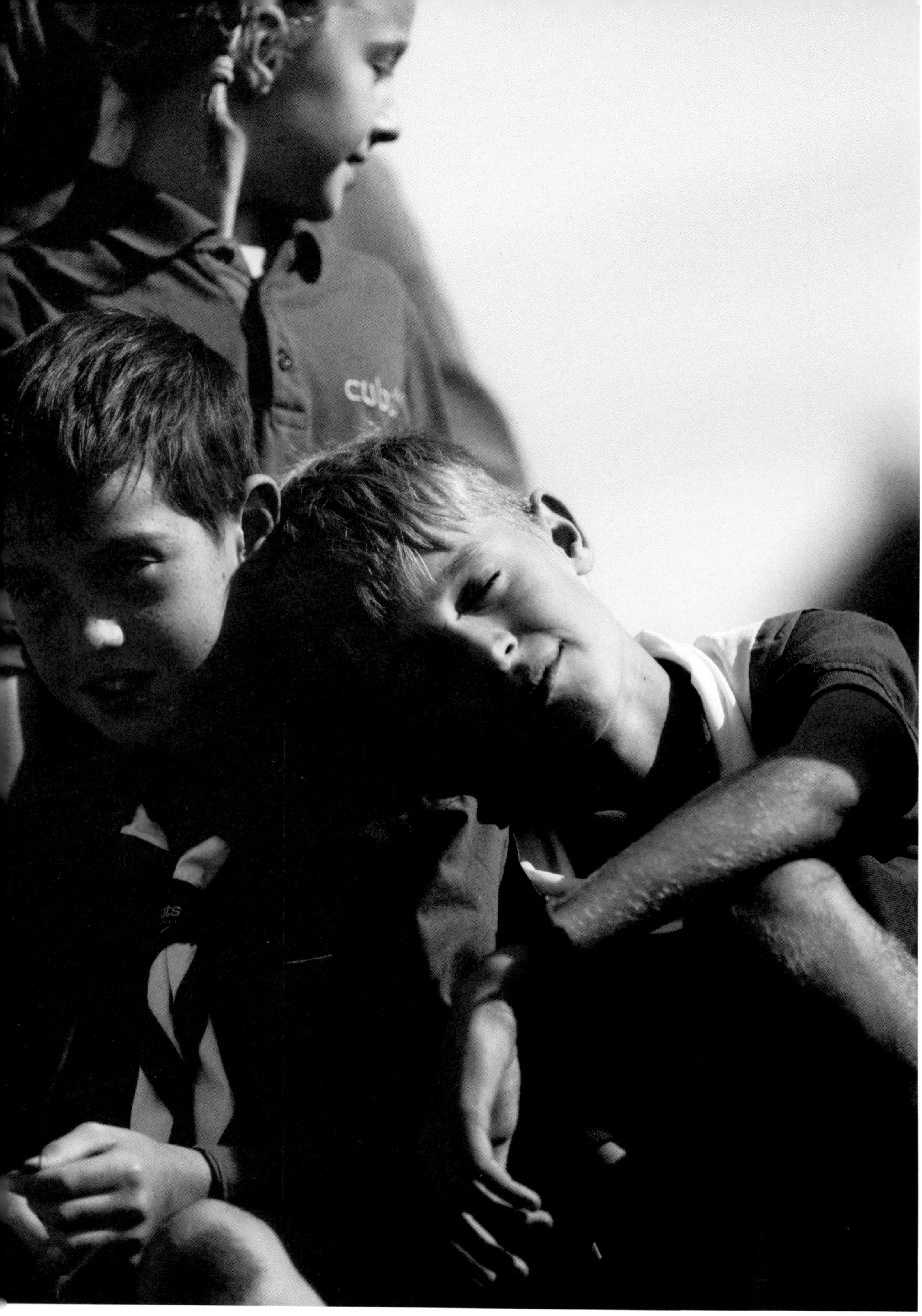

“I have played for local squash, racket ball and football teams.”

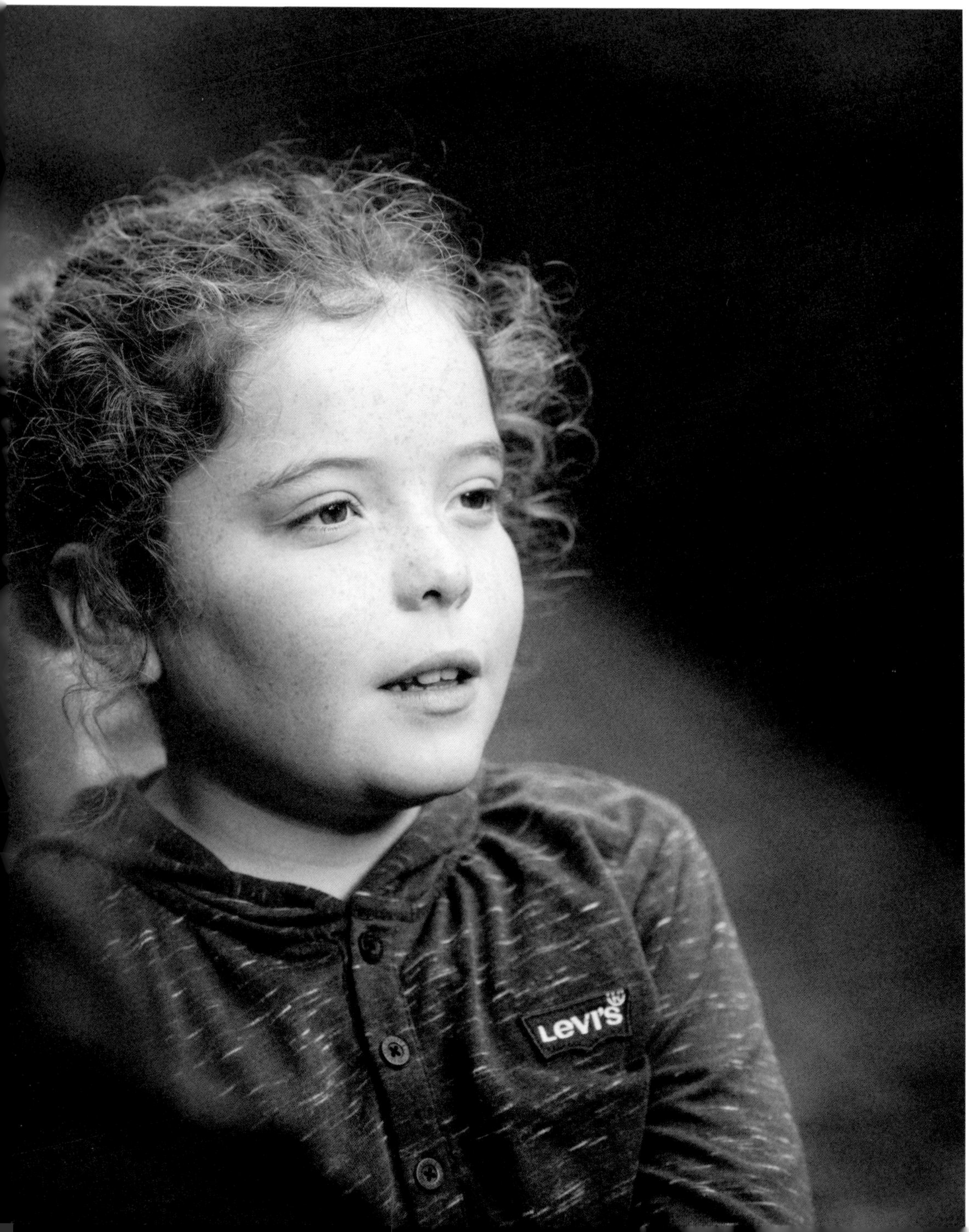

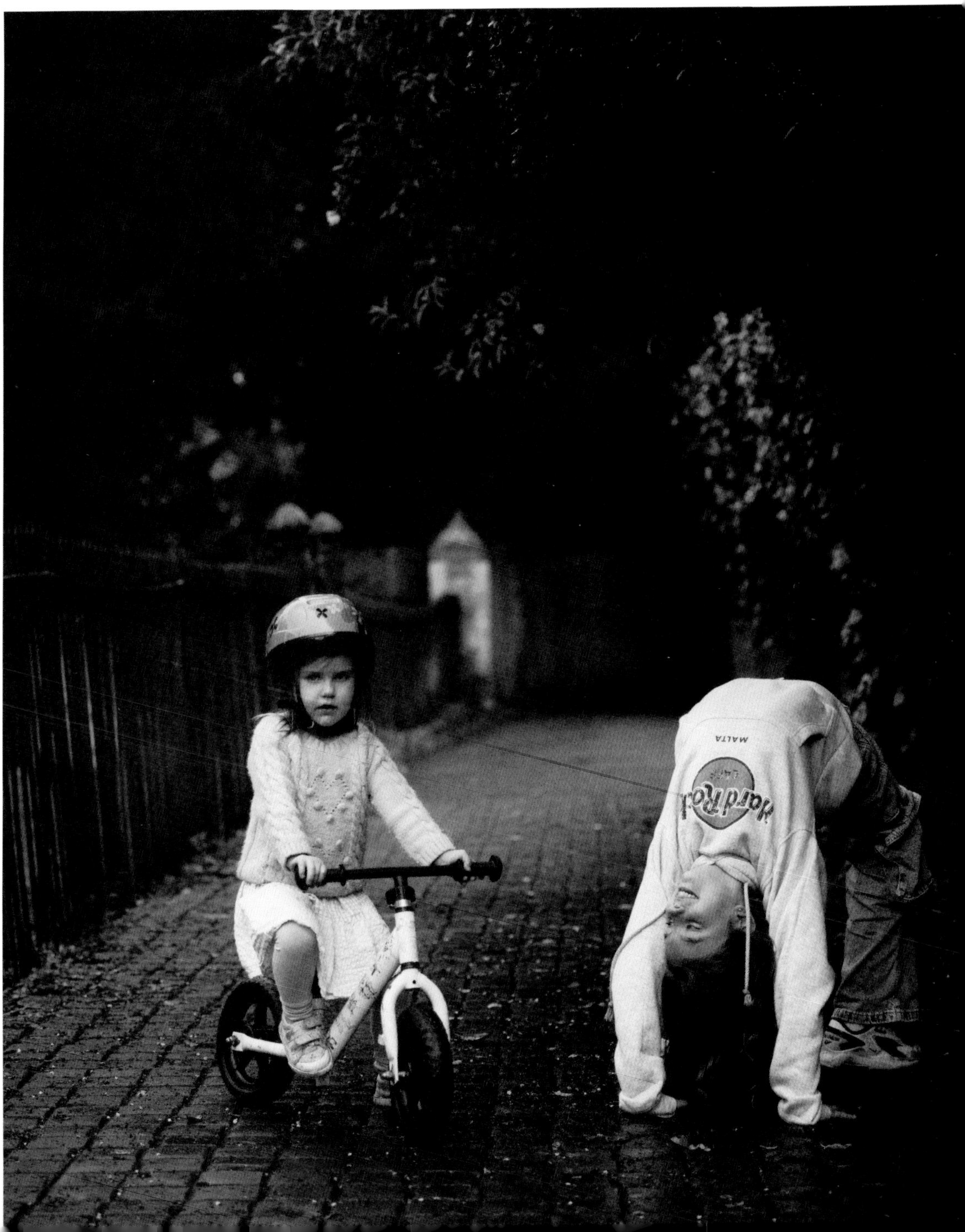
Hard Rock
MALTA

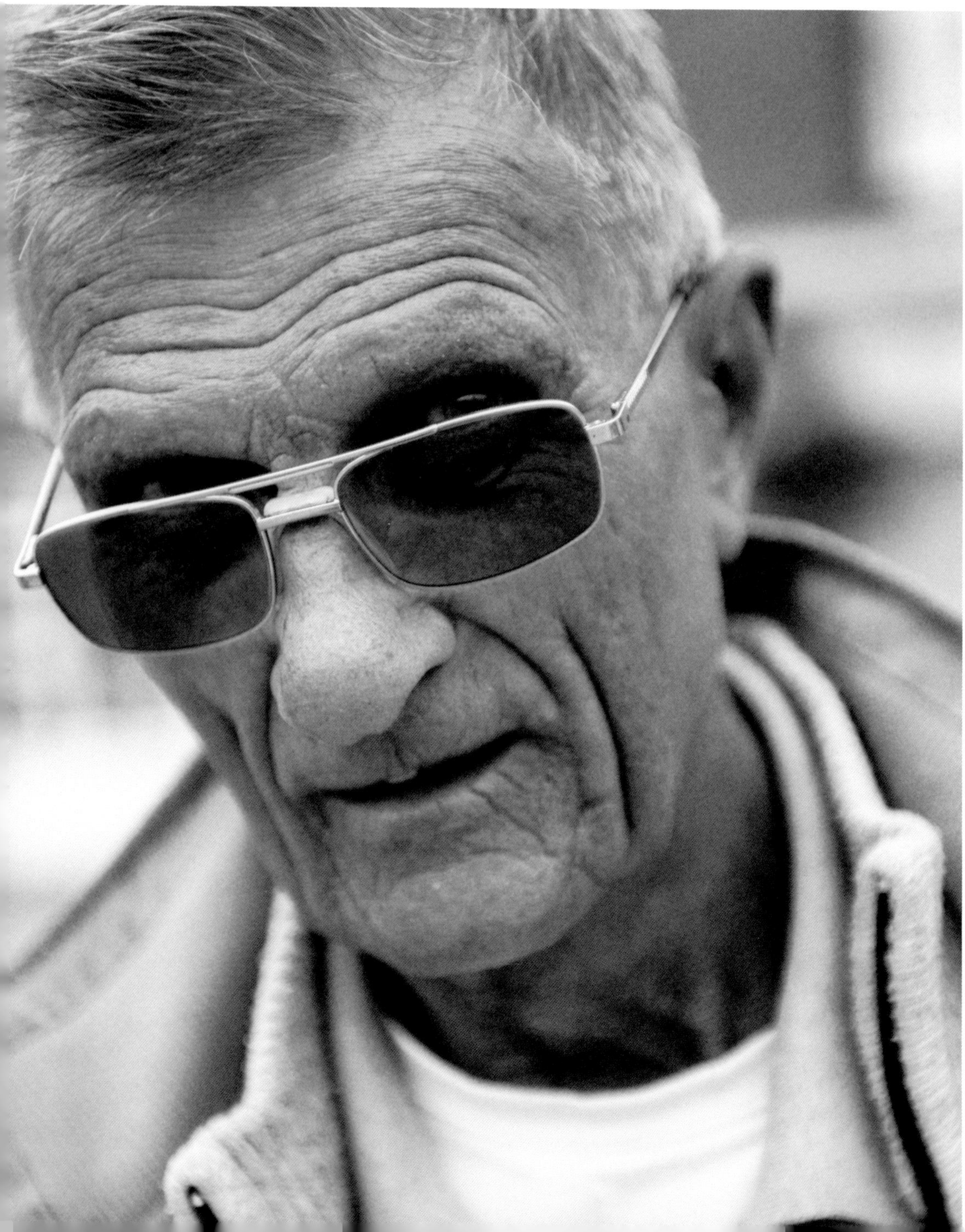

Artist Biographies

Theo Clinkard

Theo Clinkard is based in Devon and works internationally as a choreographer, theatre designer, performer, mentor and teacher. He launched his dance company in 2012 and has steadily built a reputation for creating affecting and visually arresting contemporary work that centres the moving body. Theo works with attention, the senses and the imagination as a way to generate and articulate a landscape of feelings, creating opportunities for memorable connection between audiences, dancers and participants. Theo is an Associate Artist at Brighton Dome, an Honorary Fellow at Plymouth University and choreographic commissions include Tanztheater Wuppertal Pina Bausch, Danza Contemporanea de Cuba & Candoco.

Camilla Greenwell

Camilla Greenwell is a director and photographer who grew up in Leeds and is based in London. She studied Fine Art at Central Saint Martins College of Art and Design before completing a postgraduate diploma in Photography at the London College of Communication. Over the past decade she has worked with numerous artists and clients to create imagery that stems from an interest in people and the stories they tell, often occupying a space between reality and performance and with a focus on movement. In 2020 she put together her first solo exhibition, *Movement in Still Form,* commissioned by Sadler's Wells. Her second solo exhibition at Déda, *Of Stillness and Sight,* included her first film *In Search of Sanctuary,* commissioned by James Cousins Company.

Ruth Quayle

Ruth Quayle is the author of 15 books for children, including the much-loved *Magnificent Mabel* series. She grew up surrounded by sisters (she's the middle of three) and spent a lot of her childhood writing to the tooth fairy, pretending she had a pet rabbit and stomping up to her room to read books - vital training for a children's author. She lives in a small village near Oxford with her husband and three children.

Will Burns

Will Burns was born in London and lives in Buckinghamshire. His first full poetry collection *Country Music* was published with Offord Road Books in 2020 and won the Laurel Prize for Best First Collection. His debut novel *The Paper Lantern* was published in July 2021 with Weidenfeld & Nicholson for which he was named as one of The Observer's Top 10 Debut Novelists of 2021. In 2019 he released *Chalk Hill Blue* a collaborative album made with the composer Hannah Peel, which set his poems to her music.

Claire Fuller

Claire Fuller is the author of five novels. Her latest, *The Memory of Animals* was published in April 2023. Her previous *Unsettled Ground* won the Costa Novel Award and was shortlisted for the Women's Prize for Fiction. Her books have been translated into more than 20 languages. Claire also writes flash fiction and short stories. Many have been published, and she has won the BBC Opening Lines short story competition, and the Royal Academy / Pin Drop prize. She has taught creative writing including short stories and flash fiction to a huge range of people of differing abilities, and has judged both short story and flash fiction writing competitions.

Village was commissioned and produced by Bucks Culture as part of its season STORIES in autumn 2024. (charity number: 1196317).

Village photography project was conceived by Theo Clinkard Dance with photography by Camilla Greenwell. *Village* writers were commissioned by Bucks Culture.

Village was financially supported by Arts Council England, Abderrahim Crickmay Charitable Settlement, Rothschild Foundation, Buckinghamshire Council, Aylesbury Community Board, Beeches Community Board, Haddenham and Waddesdon Community Board and Burnham Foundation, with in-kind support from Burnham Parish Council, Brill Parish Council and Coldharbour Parish Council.

With much gratitude to the participating communities, parish councils, local clubs, groups and businesses in the villages Fairford Leys, Burnham and Brill.

The *Village* team was:
Lallie Davis—Director, Bucks Culture
Ursula White—Stories Engagement Producer
Eckhard Thiemann—Creative Associate
Rosalind Conlon—Producer, Theo Clinkard Dance
Production Management—Mat Ort, Dom Martin, Linsey Hall.
Choreography Assistants—Alice Ortona Coles, Ana Noakes, Elisa de la Luz Irsara, Fionn Cox-Davies, Quincey Kawahara, Ruby Wenham.
Photography Assistants—Damien Hockey, Bella Galliano-Hale.
With special thanks to—Reverend Gemma Beesley, Cllr Andrew Cole, Andy Fisher, Keith Gray, Cllr Marie Hammon, Adam Killeya , Viv Nicholas, Shirley Shaw, Cllr Liz Springs, Cllr Steve Wadlow, Imaan Yasin.

buckinghamshireculture.org

BUCKS CULTURE

BUCKS CULTURE STORIES

9 781036 906054